Chestnut Review

VOLUME 4
2022–2023

Second Edition

Chestnut Review
Ithaca, New York
https://chestnutreview.com

Chestnut Review appears four times a year online, in January, April, July, and October, and once per year in print in July.

ISSN 2688-0350 (online)
ISSN 2688-0342 (print)
ISBN 978-1-965158-03-6

Chestnut Review

CONTENTS

Year Four in Review

Year Four was a benchmark for us: the year in which we broke one thousand submissions per month. Staffing wise, of course, this meant many more readers were needed, and we quickly saw ourselves moving to having multiple editors and associate editors in the two sides of the house (poetry and prose) to handle this load. We also debuted our new feedback option at the editorial level for writers who wanted pointed critique from our editor-level staff.

From our success at the AWP Philadelphia conference, we expanded in 2023 in Seattle to a booth, and saw increased visitations and meet-ups with our writers, artists, and submitters.

In January, 2023, we also inaugurated a project which the pandemic had delayed: our first-ever in-person retreat. Twelve writers joined us in Mérida, Mexico for a week, many with partners, giving us a group of 20 in all. They participated in intensive workshops, both critique and generative, and took in the fabulous weather and culture of the Yucatan peninsula for a full week. Our second retreat, to Wales in the summer, also was a great success, with a different vibe from Mexico. We stayed at the National Writing Centre of Wales (Ty Newydd) and enjoyed the unusual boon of unrelenting sunshine with our fourtee-strong writer cohort. Both of our retreats reaffirmed our desire to create more opportunities for community with our growing network of writers and artists.

Our chapbook team continued apace, producing four excellent offerings from Sue Mell (*Giving Care*), Sara Siddiqui Chansarkar (*Skin Over Milk*), Esperanza Cintrón (*Boulders: Detroit Nature Poems*), and Seif-Eldeine (*Voices from a Forgotten Letter*). We committed to an increased publication schedule of four chaps per year, to essentially align with our issues. We also made the decision to end the chapbook contest in favor of two open reading periods per year.

In awards, once again, we had a winner in 2023 Best Small Fictions: Subhravanu Das saw his lovely "The Many Uses of a Banyan Tree" selected, while two of our visual artists, Kathleen Frank and Biswamohini Dhal, had their artwork chosen as finalists for Best of the Net.

Year Four Statistics

5/15/2022-5/14/2023

Submissions received:
12,001

Pieces Published:
78
(20 prose, 20 art, 36 poetry, 2 contest)

Acceptance rate:
.65%

Chestnut Review
VOLUME 4 NUMBER 1 SUMMER 2022
FOR STUBBORN ARTISTS

COVER ART

Patrick van Raalten
"Fluidity"
Digital Art, May 10, 2021

I created this artwork called "Fluidity" as a visual representation of our always changing lives. It is a beautiful reminder that nothing is set in stone. You, as a human being, are always transforming from one state to another.

Chestnut Review

VOLUME 4 NUMBER 1 SUMMER 2022

Chestnut Review LLC, Ithaca, New York
chestnutreview.com

Chestnut Review appears four times a year online, in January, April, July, and October, and once per year in print in July.

ISSN 2688-0350 (online), ISSN 2688-0342 (print)

CONTENTS

Introduction

Welcome to Summer, a new beginning and a fourth cycle that we are so pleased to complete with all of you. Our print edition of Volume 3 will be out this month, and we've also just published two prose chapbooks that we are delighted to share with you from last summer's contest: Sue Mell's *Giving Care* and Sara Siddiqui Chansarkar's *Skin Over Milk* which features cover art by Oormila Vijayakrishnan Prahlad. As prose chapbook editor, I had the pleasure of interviewing Sue and Sara together to feature their chapbooks and celebrate them in this issue, and I hope to make a digital version of the full video interview available on our site and social media soon. Our staff and I look forward to reading the submissions this year and curating excellent work.

Summer is a time to stretch, relax, and grow with confidence. We are growing, slowly and resolutely, piloting opportunities to engage with our audience and the broader world. Yet it is hard these days to ignore the escalating crises in our world and the small- and large-scale tragedies taking place. At times like these, art is a vital act of resistance and acknowledgement—of both the ways of the world, and how we envision those ways changing. We take solace in our community, which includes you. Please take the time to stretch, relax, and savor the works on these pages, leaves on the *Chestnut* tree.

SUE MELL

WINNER OF THE 2021 PROSE CHAPBOOK CONTEST

In *Giving Care*, Sue Mell delivers short, sharp and powerfully rendered essays on caregiving a parent in decline. Mell navigates the shifting mother-daughter boundaries along a complicated past, the relentless present with its crises and consequences, and on toward the inevitable future never far from view. Written with lyrical control, humor and truth at the core, Mell's essays reveal a kind of grief that infiltrates further with each terrible task, while revealing each terrible task as a profound act of love.

—Stephanie Gangi, acclaimed novelist of *The Next* and *Carry the Dog*

After a catastrophic fall, broken bones, and months of rehab, Sue Mell's mother returned home with her adult daughter—"dogged fixer, belated stepper-in"—as full-time caregiver. Leaving her career and independent life in San Francisco, Mell finds her days filled with the logistics of cleaning blood off a carpet runner, having a hospital bed delivered, dealing with home health aides. With the onset of Covid, her world becomes ever smaller: her mother's house, wistful glimpses of the trees and birds outside, a "violent smear of music" from a passing car. *Giving Care* is a brief yet resonant collection that captures the quiet intimacy of caregiving in a series of vivid snapshots. Powerful, truthful, and never sentimental, it's a tour through the world of a child turned adult and an adult returning to childhood.

—Kathryn Kulpa, author of *Girls on Film*

For everyone worried about easing their mother's decline, or about how their kids will handle their own decline, or what they'll do without kids when the time comes, Sue Mell's *Giving Care* is a box of bittersweet chocolates. One brief moment after another captured in urgent flashes, beautifully expressing what it's like to keep going through moments dark and light in parental tending, hoping each day for our favorite flavor, that this one will be a good one.

—Allison K Willams, author of *Seven Drafts*

Resistance

In the shared room of the rehab facility, a freestanding closet with cheap veneer snags the privacy curtain. I reach, I jump, swinging the bulky fabric around until it releases. We are wrapped in seclusion, my mom on protest today: refusing to let me turn on the light, to read to her, to watch a movie or nature videos on my iPad.

Now she's refusing to eat, not wanting to go on, though her physical recovery is astonishingly good. More than once, she's asked that I "pull the plug." But there's no plug to pull, only Percocet and another three weeks until her bones knit back together. Then six more daunting, tedious weeks of physical therapy to get her walking again.

Her notion to stop eating? Not a realistic plan. I resist telling her, this woman who cringes at the sound of a chair being scraped across the floor, the painful process of actual starvation. But what do I know of her terror? Of her failing memory? The knowledge that she is less and less who she was?

Across the room, another curtain is swept closed as the woman recovering so well from a stroke suffers a sudden drop in blood pressure that will send her back to the hospital. My mom, without her hearing aid in, is unaware. But I hear the panic and confusion of language between the woman's visiting friend and the nurse's aide, the shift supervisor and the orderly, all scrambling to help. I beg and cajole, asking my mom what result she expects from her melodramatic protest. I get teary, I get mad, and lose patience. "This is bullshit," I say, resorting to the indignant banner-cry of my thirteen-year-old self.

She looks at me then, her eyes without her glasses open and vulnerable. "Oh, honey bear," she says. And when food service brings her dinner tray, my mom wolfs down her soup.

A Conversation with Sue Mell and Sara Siddiqui Chansarkar, Prose Chapbook Winner and Finalist

NB: This conversation has been truncated and is available in full on *Chestnut Review's* website; tune in for chapbook writing advice, more discussion of the writing life, and extra details.

MP: Hello everyone! Today I'm here with our prose chapbook 2021 winner Sue Mell and our finalist Sara Siddiqui Chansarkar. Thank you for taking the time to meet and I'm so thrilled that the two of you get to engage with each other as well. When I read both of your chapbooks for the first time in the queue I was just blown away, I knew I had something special on my hands, and it's really been wonderful to work with both of you during the editing process. I'm so happy that these works are in the world now.

So first, I would like to pose a getting-to-know you question, which are three tropes, themes or obsessions that keep coming up in your writing.

SM: The three things that tend to drive my work are loss, grief, and mortality. But a lighter note I would definitely say that music and art are themes that run through it as well as the life of inanimate objects.

MP: Exactly. I think all those things are found to some extent in *Giving Care*. What about you, Sara?

SSC: Mine would be gender parity, feminism, and relationships in general, familial or otherwise. And being an immigrant and a writer of color, the feminism I bring forward is not a loud but a silent and resilient kind of feminism that is in women who try to improve lives around them while still doing their duty, which is definitely in my chapbook.

MP: Absolutely! As soon as you said those three things, I thought, "that's the chap." I also think it's interesting that those themes are present in *Giving Care*, feminism as a quiet duty, pushing against expectations quietly. I love the way these chapbooks resonate around this idea of what family relationships should be like.

I'm wondering whether these chapbooks were built intentionally as cohesive projects or if the actual flash lead you to the idea that this could be a chapbook?

SSC: I did not plan on this being a chapbook. I just wrote the story "Skin Over Milk" and I had wanted to write something about rain because monsoon is such a phenomenon in India that I just go back to my childhood whenever I hear the rain. I was just writing about life in a house like that and I just don't know where that milk and tea came from. That story was just three hundred words and it got shortlisted for a prize and I thought, okay, maybe there's something there, so I took stories about the ripe mango and earpiercing that I'd published before and conceived the story of these sisters who live in this house, and that grew and grew. I just kept adding stories to it while preserving the collective voice of "we." Once I realized I had ten chapters, I submitted it to *Chestnut Review* and of course in editing it became twelve chapters.

SM: Wow, that's amazing!

MP: What about you, Sue?

SM: It started with "Interval" which I had sent to *Cleaver Magazine* and prior to this, I had been working on the revision a novel for a year and taking care of my mom so I needed something small and manageable. All that time I was thinking of things and scrawling a note here and there. My original idea was to do a collection of pieces about my mom and then try to leverage that into a bigger book. But I realized I didn't necessarily want to spend all the time a book would take since I was living in it. That's when I decided to order it sequentially and submit it as a chapbook.

MP: With you having come from a novel and knowing how long it is, I respect that you could acknowledge that. These chaps have a searing intensity to them that conveys the complexity of a novel. I'm so honored that we get to publish the final product.

SM: The changes that we made working together really elevated the work. I could not be happier.

SSC: I totally agree, Maria. All your edits and the loose ends I had flying around, that we finally tied them up, I'm just so thankful for that.

MP: Thank you both, and I'm so glad that we could publish both of your chaps. The editing process was amazing and these were works we really wanted to publish. So Sue, you have a novel coming out soon. Could you tell us what *Provenance* is about in a nutshell?

SM: It's being published by Madville Publishing, and you can find it on Bookshop or Amazon. Here's the description: "Still grieving his wife's early death, DJ has spent the last three years-and the money from her insurance policy-collecting guitars, composing music, and continuing to shop the Brooklyn stoop sales and flea markets they'd always enjoyed. When his building is sold, he takes refuge in his younger sister's half-finished basement, imagining a comfortable and solitary retreat in Hurley, the small Hudson Valley town where they grew up. Instead, he finds himself caught up in her troubling divorce, drafted as caregiver for his 11-year-old niece, and unable to face or afford a storage unit crammed with hundreds of vinyl records and every other scrap of his former life. DJ gifts his niece a marbled glass egg, a porkpie hat, and one of his prized guitars. But what's asked of him, on his return to Hurley is not to give the perfect object-it's to give of himself."

SSC: It sounds amazing!

MP: Sara, specifically for you. You have a collection, *Morsels of Purple*, which is a collection of flash stories. I know you are prolific and active in the literary community; you publish a lot and you have a full-time job and other commitments too. Here at *Chestnut* we support stubborn writers and encourage people to have the grit to keep writing and get published. I'm wondering what your process is like.

SSC: For me, I write flash because I don't have time for a bigger work. I have a full-time job and I haven't been trained in writing; I have always been a reader so all I know about writing comes from that. In Sue's chapbook, microwaving the applesauce for nine seconds stood out for me so much because my writing is like that. When I have nine seconds to myself in the shower or some quiet time that's when things I've seen, read, interactions with people, those come back and the kernel of the story is born. And that's why it stood out because before everything else starts, that miniscule time to think, that's where my stories come from.

For submissions, I don't have a regular process but I see sometimes that I need to write more stories to have something to submit. You see the external success but really those stories have been waiting in the submission queue for months, sometimes, and there are days when I want to pull my hair and say, "What am I doing?"

MP: I think a lot of people see the success on the outside and don't realize the hard work that's underneath. Sara, I also love that you reminded us of the nine second thing because it's so powerful. I think it's a great analogy for the process. You fit the writing into the time you have.

SM: And sometimes having more time is your enemy.

MP: For sure! Our last question is about the future. What's next for you? That could be as simple as getting rest—
SM: (laughs)

MP: Or anything that you want to do next.

SM: When I finished my fellowship, I had a bunch of stories that I had published early on in my writing career and I wanted to make a collection. I wrote into the secondary characters and fleshed out the second half of the book. I'm now sending that work out and also submitting some of the individual stories from within there. Then I'm trying to start a new project in collage format—like Emily St. John Mandel's *The Glass Hotel*. Unlike my other work it has more focus on friendship than romantic relationships or family. Some days I'd love to do something completely new and I'm not sure what that is yet.

SSC: I have been writing a novel that I just drop for months, but I'm hoping to get through one draft to figure out what I need to do next. Also, a couple people who have read *Skin Over Milk* have said they want to know more about what happens to these characters, a second chapbook or even a novel. So that's in my mind now, too!

MP: Thank you both so much. It's been such a pleasure. I would be thrilled to see any of these works in the world.

Sue Mell's *Giving Care* and Sara Siddiqui Chansarkar's *Skin Over Milk* are now available for sale on our website and at Amazon.com.

chestnutreview.com/books

Giving Care

Sue Mell

Skin Over Milk
Sara Siddiqui Chansarkar

Next Page: Oormila Vijayakrishnan Prahlad's cover art

MICHELLE HULAN

The Universe, as in One Last Song for the Lonely Hearts

I believe the blackest hole is the one we inhabit
—Eugenio Montale

Imagine a time before morning. When light was just fire bending into space. Imagine when the Universe unfolded like a silk cloth in the wind, singing and building life the way a child makes puppets from socks: clumsily sewing carbon to oxygen and nitrogen to hydrogen then pushing its hand up your throat. Our Universe isn't gentle, but it sang us into existence. Even everything wants something else sometimes. But these days, the lines around our eyes curve like comets. Our hearts beat like dying stars. Like the Universe, we are destined to end. To become black holes chasing after each other. Our bones making kin with weasels and ivy and mirth and rust in the blackest one. We will haunt space like mist over lakes. It will certainly be the closest we've ever been, and we will be singing:

I remember life.
There was so much. I held it
all. I held it all.

Cataloging Ghosts

My favorite family myth involves my grandfather being awoken by brawling ghosts. But before I tell it to you, you need to understand that by the age of fifteen, Carlos—my grandfather whom I never met—had been tossed from household to household in indentured servitude because his mother couldn't guarantee dinner every night. So at the time of this haunting, he was working at a worn-down corn mill in Antigua, Guatemala, waking at around three in the morning to prepare the flour for breakfast tortillas. Either because he had no choice or saw no purpose in returning home for a few hours, he slept in a makeshift room on the second floor of the mill. He tried making it a home, adorning the walls with posters of long-dead musicians like Pedro Infante, but his decorations couldn't hide his desire to break free from those four walls.

One night, already in bed, Carlos heard fighting in the attic above him. I imagine he heard punches whiff through the air, with boxing shoes rattling the floorboards, before their echoing impact cascaded dust from the overhead rafters. I don't know how many lips have molded this story since the first time it was told. In the still of night, I don't know if he could have noticed dust spilling from the ceiling. Perhaps he started sneezing or his eyes burned, or maybe the moon bloomed full and distant starlight bled into that tiny room. I just know he heard something crash through the ceiling, and he ran outside before his aching soles reminded him of the shoes he left at his bedside.

He didn't have anywhere else to run off to, so he couldn't have gone too far. Close enough to return by morning, sunlight weeping through the window frame. He found nothing. The ceiling was intact, and dust still littered the floorboards in the attic above, undisturbed. He never slept in the room again. Though it may have been a wild animal or some nightmare disguised as his reality, every time the story is told, those creatures who make noise are called ghosts.

~

We often use ghosts as scapegoats; it's a convenient label to toss onto the inexplicable.

~

Ghosting is a term used whenever a person in a relationship seems to disappear. No calls, no texts; their absence whispers goodbye. I don't feel that we need to justify or announce every departure, but I find myself wanting to have this conversation whenever it happens to me. Every romance I've taken part in ends with a sudden cease of communication. I try not to be anxious about it—we're adults and busy and need our space—but the moment someone takes longer than usual to reply, I brace myself for it. The hole their absence will create.

~

Most media I've seen depict ghosts as impressions of their living form, just transparent or with their bottom half missing; occasionally, a cartoonish entity that looks like a marshmallow or a sheet with holes for eyes. I haven't pictured a form for myself after I'm gone, but I expect to be free from the shackles of my skin. I wouldn't mind incomprehensible shapes or winged angels; I'd love to shine with the colors of starlight. Whichever shape I may take, I cannot wait to become a ghost. Don't worry, dear reader; I am not looking forward to dying, I just think being an incorporeal entity unbound by shallow ideas of gender and labor sounds like a more pleasant experience than living.

~

While I'm writing this first draft, my best friend has been replying to my messages about once a day. Well, it's more like she sends me a message about something happening to her before ignoring anything I send back. Through high school, college, and half a decade, we grew up and grew closer only to swiftly fall into silence. It's nothing, really. I can step back and shake the figure standing in my place, telling them they're overreacting, clingy, codependent. Even so, I don't enjoy carrying this feeling. I don't want to idly sit by, watching our futures ghost away.

~

My father once stepped into a museum and was confronted with a portrait of Pedro de Alvarado y Contreras—the man who led the colonial conquest of Guatemala. Because of its commonality, I wasn't concerned when I realized we shared a last name; however, dread creeped in after he mentioned how much the portrait looked like his own father. It's been hundreds of years, so nobody in our family believes we're connected to him, but it's a frightening, intrusive thought to imagine my bloodline being responsible for restless spirits lying in the Guatemalan soil.

~

When I was nine years old, I huddled around the tiny monitor of my cousin's computer, watching YouTube videos "confirming" the existence of ghosts. Those were the years when the loading time was longer than the video itself, when I idolized older boys and mimicked their movements, when my cousins bullied me enough to avoid Guatemala for half a decade—but for one shining moment, the oldest cousin called me to the dining room because he had something cool to show me. I pulled a chair up beside him and watched dashcam footage of a truck driver slamming his breaks after a pale specter manifested before the windshield. Since the camera caught it, it must've been real.

~

Months after we broke up, my ex-girlfriend returned a sweater I lent her. I was still nineteen, listening to *Blonde* and *Twin Fantasy* religiously. When I returned home, I held the sweater in my arms as if hugging a ghost. Its scent was strong enough to almost convince me the relationship wasn't all that bad, and years later, I would accidentally buy detergent that was strong enough to remind me that it was. I don't remember missing her in those months, but if the room was ever quiet enough, I would notice, just outside my periphery, the ghosts of the people we once were.

~

My father tells me hauntings aren't as common anymore because we're so occupied by everything else, we don't notice the paranormal around us. Sometimes he's referring to how distracted we are by our phones, but other times he's describing how we seem to have lost touch with a world just out of reach.

~

While revising this essay, my best friend calls me and we speak as if nothing happened because nothing happened. There was no weight behind her absence. I carry shame in grieving something not even lost, but anticipation can hurt more than the inevitable wound.

~

It's taken over twenty years for my father to catalog his ghosts. He's a writer in secret, and the only project he's undertaken in my lifetime is a linear narrative of how we came to be. He's writing about our family. He claims to always be working on the final draft, and that the only thing keeping him from finalizing it is his bank account. He loves reading, but doesn't read. He loves writing, but rarely writes. His manuscript was going to be my graduation present in high school, but it wasn't ready before my bachelor's degree arrived in the mail. It's still in its final draft. His ghosts have unfinished business.

~

My family tree casts a shadow I'll never see the edges of. I cannot name anyone older than my grandparents on either side, and even then, I don't know them as if they were people. I don't know if I'll ever have great grandchildren—and even if I do, I cannot know if they will ever learn my name.

~

After the first "final" draft of this essay, months away from being twenty-two, and in a pub in Chicago, I glance at my best friend as she speaks with her friends who I've only just met. We haven't crossed the threshold into acquaintances yet, so they feel like friendly strangers. I understand the workplace gossip from repeated names, but it doesn't stop me from being the ghost in the room. My eyesight is clear, but my presence slips from my body until I'm left Kubrick-staring at the saltshaker at the edge of the table.

My best friend asks if I'm okay and I nod because I'm not about to tell her that my dissociation is acting up again—as it always does—and this time, it makes me wonder whether I'm still asleep in Texas, dreaming of conversations that I will never be a part of. It doesn't feel like I am in the state of Illinois, much less in a lonely pub filled with the noises of televisions talking over each other and muted conversations. She looks back to her friends.

Weeks later, I'll find the words to explain to her how I feel, but I'll tell you now: Dripping wet from the evening's rainfall and hungry but not starving—I am a camera. Unobtrusive and only here to capture the moment.

~

Time has passed and I no longer worry about the stability of our friendship, but I dread the relationships I'll create in the future. This isn't the first time an absence has created an avalanche. I've shattered relationships with the desire of coming closer; a possession doesn't work without a host. I've wanted to live in another person's skin. To cut a hole in their chest and crawl inside. I thought this pandemic convinced me I could survive on my own, but when do I not carry somebody else on my mind?

~

An unkept spirit doesn't need much to keep going. An altar in the corner of a bedroom. A place to sleep and dream. Some food. A way to pass the time. I want to love and be loved, but it's easier to assume the worst than to trust. Sometimes, it's easier to haunt than to live.

~

Writing nonfiction is a process of cataloging ghosts. Either literally in discussing those who have already passed, or figuratively in bracing for our eventual departure. I'm here, alive and writing, but unsure if I'll still be breathing once you're reading this. Writing is a call to a void, demanding an echo. Writing is a ghost in the doorway, hoping you'll turn around.

~

I choose to believe in ghosts. Objects graced with the presence of a loved one always feel heavier; and once they're gone, I choose to believe the weight of their actions still affects the soil. There's something comforting in knowing the afterlife is closer to our world than we think.

I choose to imagine my grandfather knows who I am. He died before he could learn I was named after him, but maybe he's aware of my presence in a different shape or form.

I choose to believe in myself, who haunts but tries to do better. I want to love without possession; I want to shake the table and release the tension in the water. I want to trust and find the strength to command my body in the morning. I want to sleep.

WILLIAM C. CRAWFORD

"Yellow Purse"

Digital Photo Shot in Chicago using Forensic Foraging, 2021

I developed Forensic Foraging, a throwback, minimalist technique for modern digital photographers. I seek to uncover the often hidden uniqueness found in everyday mundane subjects. When properly presented in an image, the seemingly trivial can become pleasing eye candy.

windmills over Zaandam

alone on the street
there are men saying things to you
in a language that you wish was foreign,
but it's not
and you want to dive
in canals of trash water
to make yourself feel clean
and the smoke gathers in your throat
to cut like knives—
this place doesn't want to hear your voice—
but you are screaming poetry in a restaurant
and all your friends inhale plants on fire
and cry
and did you know there are fields of open space
here
where human hands haven't groped yet
and a woman is pulling ribbon
out of her own body
until these men remember they are children
that they don't want to be
and when you catch the train
downtown in the morning
a man makes you a waffle
covered in ripe fruits

and you eat it on the stones outside,
consuming color
like you are the only thing
that belongs inside of you.

SASHA WADE

Intercession

Do concerned birds see everything
we can't? Like a low-flying starling

starved in winter, I peck holes of daylight
into night's half-frozen dirt, refusing

to excuse that I failed to punch through
clouds, pluck my son before his feet flew

off the skateboard—back arched in the air.
And what of the tree-tops: did they cavern

his screams into the wind's sail, or catch
his face—the shock, plummeting

out of boyhood—mouth half-open
to the sun? If I tell you what I saw hours

later in his eyes, when he whispered,
"I don't want to die," if I tell you how close

the sky came to settling beneath him
would you believe in trumpets, tired angels,

sword-snapping dragons crowding the moon?
When the surgeon told my son he'd lost

a patient weeks earlier—same accident
same age—I watched their mirrored faces,

drops of clear shrapnel singing their cheek-skin.
I saw streaming and surrender, too, like the flock

of swans outside the hospital window—necks
bent from battle—frayed feathers cushioning

gravel-snow below. I saw what the birds saw
weeks earlier—same accident, same age, no angel.

Our Trespassing

I was the only one who protested when they painted over the tennis courts. I remember the morning well because of the way the cool air kept memories of fall tournaments in my periphery, while the rising sun promised radical change in the afternoon. It would've been the perfect morning to hit. The parking lot was empty, and no neighbors lined up beneath the clear blue sky with their rackets and balls, no children played on the playground beside the club. The neighborhood was quiet, save for the swish of workers' strokes. I stood silently and watched as the men decorated their pants in speckles of blue, red, and white—their bright yellow vests spoiling the national aesthetic. Slowly but surely, the service boxes beneath their feet disappeared into three-point arcs and free throw lines.

My peaceful demonstration wasn't much of a display. I didn't bring a sign, or chant, or yell. I just stood on the sidewalk and watched the men do their work. My intention wasn't to make them uncomfortable, but I'm rather certain I did. I'm not sure what my intention was. Every once in a while, one of the workers turned to another and pointed at me. Others shot a glance in my direction. They whispered and laughed. Eventually, a man with a large belly and small clipboard walked over. He smiled a knowing smile and spoke.

"Don't worry bud, they'll be ready before you know it," he said.

It took me a moment to realize that he thought I was a basketball player. Maybe his boss had told him about the vote to replace the courts. That was all the neighbors could talk about. He probably figured I was the head of their charge. The man wore a camouflage hat with the rebel flag on its front. Perhaps I didn't look like what he expected a tennis player to look like.

I shook my head.

"I'm a tennis player," I said.

I indicated towards my Roger Federer hat with the stylized *F*. I could've pointed at my Babolat shirt, or the shorts I wore that ended well above the knee. I didn't want to make him feel stupid.

"I learned to play on these courts," I clarified.

The man, the supervisor most likely, fixed me with a strange look. It seemed as though he were seeing me now for the first time.

"I see," he replied.

He turned to his clipboard, tracing his finger across the page as though trying to determine how this new bit of information might correlate with the task at hand. I suppose he realized it didn't. The supervisor shrugged.

"Sorry, bud," he said. He turned away.

I continued to stand and watch. Like I said, it wasn't much of a protest. The air was gentle, and there were no counter protestors waving *We want hoops* signs. I didn't rush onto the court and tie myself to the net or anything like that. I only wanted to pay my respects. These were the courts where my father and I played—where I learned the game and spent the happiest days of my youth. On Sunday mornings, on summer days, he and I would wake up early, before the sun rose above the trees beside the clubhouse, while the air was still cool and the morning kept its quiet. We'd spend precious hours, trading forehands and serves, like a prayer before the sermon, until my mother called us home for church. Those days were over now, with no tennis courts within walking distance. My protest was a funeral for a lifestyle lost.

After a while, I turned to head home. As I moved down the street, I heard one of the workers say, "Goddamn, finally." Another said something about "Freak." Laughter all around. Then I heard one last voice before I moved out of earshot.

"Black folk play tennis?"

I heard nothing after that. The wind laughed in my direction. I made my way home.

***

My father once said that the best athletes in this country play all of the wrong sports. It wasn't until the basketball players showed up that I realized what he meant.

They were tall and muscular, most of them. The ones that weren't sat on the sidelines. On the hottest days, they played with their shirts off, maybe because of the heat, but perhaps also so that the young ladies headed to the swimming pool might stare at the impressive tattoos and biceps on display. There were some days when even I had to marvel.

One or two of them might have been from the neighborhood, but most of them weren't. Our neighborhood stretched across multiple streets, around multiple bends, with villages that each contained many, many houses, and yet there were only three Black families in total. The basketball players were of all different shades, but the majority of them had skin like mine.

Their games were like a gospel in their intensity. A gospel with more profanity than a nun had prayers. Most looked to be my age—somewhere in their early 20s—maybe even 30s. Others looked older, a few were teens. It seemed as though their games weren't always for fun. Some days, they screamed at one another. Other days, they joked and laughed. But no matter what, they came and played. It didn't rain much that summer, but when it did, they came. Meanwhile, the neighbors hardly ventured near the courts. They were the ones who voted to have them. They were the ones who argued tennis was a dying game, and that basketball would better suit the future of this area. My father said they would've been better off building a video game center. I couldn't help but feel vindicated.

At first, I was pleasantly surprised. My protest, though ineffective it may have seemed, must have had some impact on the workers. They left up a single backboard on one side of the fence, in front of a large area of unblemished, open court where one could move and maneuver without interfering with the basketball game happening next door. I took full advantage of this. Every afternoon, I went out to hit. I was unemployed that summer—having just completed my last semester at university. The real world loomed before me—one outside of education—where interacting with the people who called innocent bystanders *freaks* and assumed the worst about people like me was par for the course. The only thing that separated me from it was my ability to create the illusion of progress with the development of my tennis strokes. Father promised me I could live at home for free, so long as I "do something."

For a long time, the basketball players and I ignored one another. We were the two fixtures inside the metal fence—the tall, muscular basketball players enjoying their pick up games, and my small, sinewy frame working on forehands. The ring of their rims interrupted the thud of the backboard, while the thwack of my backhands sat beneath the vulgarities of their trash talk. Every once in a while, a neighbor passed on the sidewalk beside the court. Most ignored the basketball players, but some recognized me.

"It's a shame, isn't it?" One man offered while I rested. Another asked me about my father and said everyone missed seeing us hit. This did not make sense to me because it was the neighbors who voted to replace the courts, not my father and I. Before leaving me to my practice, this same man nodded towards the basketball court, towards the players and their profane exertions.

"Don't worry. Tennis courts will be back in no time." He winked at me when he said this.

At the time, I didn't understand what he meant.

***

My first interaction with one of the basketball players came on a hot Wednesday afternoon. It was so hot that the benches were too sun-soaked to sit on, and the concrete, too hot to touch. The hottest day of that summer, I would imagine. Yet the players showed up in as great of numbers as ever. They played as if the intensity of their competition could overwhelm the intensity of the heat. I couldn't help but feel inspired. I stood before the backboard, swinging harder than usual, grunting louder than usual, playing as though I wanted to be the first tennis player in history to defeat a wall. By the time I took a water break, my white shorts were drenched in sweat. On the basketball court, the players slapped hands and bent over their knees. They were spent as well. Had we been competing against one another as opposed to the sun, the referee might've called it a tie.

I stood by my side of the fence while they stood beside theirs. I couldn't help but notice them noticing me. I overhead one of them observe, "This nigga out here every day." There were more murmurs and expletives. Eventually, I heard a familiar phrase.

"Didn't know niggas played tennis."

I avoided eye contact and focused on rehydrating. I heard
another voice, in so many words, speak my mind.

"Shit. You aint never heard of Venus and Serena, nigga?"

"Yeah, I heard of them."

"This nigga like Arthur Ashe or some shit."

People often compared my father to Arthur Ashe. I looked
more like a cross between Jo-Wilfred Tsonga and Gael Monfils.
I wouldn't correct them though. I didn't want any trouble. That
seemed to be what the neighbors thought the basketball players
were. Even my mother avoided the sidewalk beside the court on
her morning walks. She had never been one to condone profan-
ity. Especially in young men who looked like me.

The basketball players mumbled amongst themselves and con-
tinued to glance. My break was over. I picked up my racket and
moved to the backboard. As I began to hit, one of the players
shouted.

"Venus!"

A few of them sniggered. I ignored this and continued with
my forehands. Very soon, my silence became a challenge. The
more I ignored them, the more they yelled.

"Serena!"

"Federer!"

"Wii Sport!"

I hit harder and harder. My grunts overwhelmed their chatter.
They must have sensed my annoyance. Soon, they began to grunt
back. Some tried to mimic me, others shrieked as a small child
would, or as if they were in the bedroom making love. The more
they mocked me, the harder I hit, and the harder the ball came
back. This is why no one beats the wall. Eventually, I took a
swing and missed. The basketball players bent over one another,
trying not so hard to stifle their laughter. I turned and glared at
them. Most looked away, but one, a young man wearing all black

with a short afro and a gap between his teeth, glared back.

"You got something to say, nigga?"

I didn't have anything to say, and even if I had, I wouldn't say it. There were many of them, and I was the only neighbor out that day. The one who called out stared me down. The other players watched. I noticed his leg shaking. It seemed as though he were as nervous as I was. I couldn't risk testing his courage. My mother lectured me long ago about the things some men would do for the defense of pride.

"Don't be shy. You got something to say?"

"No, I'm sorry," I replied.

"Shit. That's what I thought. Little white talking nigga…"

I moved to the sideline and packed my things. As I passed the basketball court on the outside fence, I overheard one of the older players say to the one who'd yelled, "Yo, chill Keith." A few looked at me as though they wanted to say something, perhaps to apologize, or maybe mock me again. I didn't stay long enough to find out.

***

My mother filed a complaint that I couldn't imagine was the first. It really was all the neighbors seemed to talk about that summer—what the courts were, what the courts would be, or what the courts should've been. Many worried about their children, who they'd wanted the basketball court for in the first place, being unable to use the recreation area because of the players' daily games. These parents wondered why their dues should go up while foreigners from another zip code used the courts for free. I could hardly sympathize with this argument. During the first week after the gates re-opened, the new basketball area sat as empty as the tennis courts ever had. My father even mentioned something about a sign that went up in nearby suburbs, advertising the new court to anyone who wanted to use it. This was most likely the neighborhood association's attempt at conjuring the illusion of money well spent. I suppose they assumed that whoever showed up would look like the majority of the people who lived in the neighborhood. It's like what my father always says about assumptions.

I steered clear of the basketball court for a while. I replaced my daily tennis practice with morning jogs. I ran at least two miles every day, sometimes as many as five. My body remained thin and long, but my legs grew strong.

It did not take long for me to realize that my status in the neighborhood had changed. A lot of the adults and teenagers in the area knew me from the tennis courts, but just as many did not. Every evening, as I jogged over hills, off sidewalks, between villages in our area, I saw many of our neighbors. Many of them glared at me. Rather quickly, I deduced the reality—they thought I was one of the basketball players. To remedy this, I modified my look. I wore shorts that ended well above the knee. I shaved my knotted Afro to a tight military buzz. I even wore a shirt that read TENNIS on the front. None of these things made a difference.

"Go home!" one teenager shouted at me on a blue evening in July. He clearly didn't understand that my home was just around the corner. That he could look from his back porch and, without squinting, see mine. I wanted to tell him, but I kept running. Just as I'd known how far the basketball players would go to defend their pride against threat, I knew how far the neighbors would go to defend their home against invasion. I didn't dare fight back.

For as much as I disliked the basketball players' presence, I developed some sympathy for them, given our common dilemma. It didn't take much for me to imagine what they were going through. My father spoke of an occasion when he saw a man parked in the lot beside the court, blaring "You Belong to the City" from his vehicle while the players played. My father believed these actions were inevitable, but my mother did not. She filed another complaint.

After a while, I figured that it would be okay for me to jog past the basketball court again. I imagined the basketball players had larger matters to attend to than making fun of me, and I was right. On the first day I saw them, they all stood outside the fence, pulling at the gate. There was a lock on the outside—one that was much fancier and difficult to break than what a person might find on a high school locker. When the players saw me approach, one of them stepped forward.

"Hey, man!"

It was Keith, the same boy who'd yelled at me a few weeks before. Now, he jogged towards me, down the short grassy slope leading towards the sidewalk. His long arms flopped by his side. Behind him, the other players stood, tugging at the lock, trying different combinations, crowded together beneath the *no trespassing* sign posted on the gate. I paused my workout and waited to hear what Keith had to say. When he stopped in front of me, he spoke with a soft voice, much softer than it had been the other day, and smiled as well. I could tell that this was his form of an apology.

"Have you got the code for the lock?" he asked.

"No," I replied, because it was true.

"Damn." Keith turned towards the other players, who were now watching our interaction. He threw up his hands, as if to say "no luck," and some of them smacked the fence. Keith looked at me and shook his head.

"White folk, man. You believe this shit?" he asked.

I hesitated to answer. I thought of how my father would respond. He was the one in our family always talking about *white folk.* His grievances had always been this way, but that summer especially, there was much cause for complaint. With the videos appearing on the news, and the evening protests downtown, my father sat at the dinner table with some new revelation, some universal wisdom about *white folk* every night. His lectures preached on how *they* would do this, and *we* should do that, until the whole world was split between a *them* and an *us*. Even before the vote to replace the court, my father assured, "White folk won't never let go of their country club sport. Not for no negro game."

There was a time during my childhood when I rolled my eyes, or defended white people against my father. I argued that there was no difference between Black people and white people, and that he was racist for insisting otherwise. After these past weeks of neighbors' scowls, I wasn't so sure. Regardless, I knew how to respond.

"I know," I said, invoking my father. I shook my head and grinned. "White folk." Keith laughed at the way I said this. He smiled.

"All right, well take it easy brother."

"You, too," I replied. I supposed we were cool now.

I imagined that would be the last time I saw the basketball players. It looked as though the neighborhood had won. Simple as that.

But the next time I ran by, it wasn't the players struggling outside of the fence. It was the head of the neighborhood association—a blond woman holding a clipboard, tugging at the gate to the area. There was a crude, makeshift lock on the fence, and the old one was gone. The woman looked exasperated. The basketball players were nowhere to be found. When I drew close, she turned towards me with a snarl.

"Do you know who did this?" she asked.

I shook my head and kept running. I could see her watching

me as I moved down the road. She drew out her cellphone and dialed a number. As far away as the next block, I could hear her yelling at someone.

"…then they cry about oppression…"

I turned the corner.

***

When they stationed a police officer in the parking lot beside the courts, I thought it would be safe to use the backboard again. The basketball players wouldn't bother me, and the neighbors, finally appeased, would leave me alone.

It was on a beautiful afternoon, with few clouds in the sky, children playing on the playground, and a number of cars outside of the clubhouse, that I made my return. I headed to the court that day with racket and balls in tow—wearing my short shorts and short hair. When I arrived at the recreation area, I saw the police officer sitting in her car with the windows rolled up, looking down at her phone. She glanced up at a white father shooting free throws with his son, but seemed uninterested in her current assignment. She made eye contact with me as I passed. When I turned toward the gate, her door opened.

"Hey, wait."

I turned around. The police officer waved me back. She wore a look that discouraged disobedience.

"What village do you live in?" she demanded.

"Westcreek," I replied. When the officer heard my voice, she looked surprised. Then she relaxed. I spoke quietly, with a different dialect than the basketball players, and I think this took her off guard.

The officer didn't even check her device to see whether I told the truth.

"You're good," she said.

I made my way towards the courts. They looked more like they did on the day I watched those workers finish them than they ever had since. The neighborhood must have had them repainted. The red, white, and blue looked fresh—with the basketball players' scuff marks and sweat stains all but erased. I imagine the neighborhood association wanted to forget the players altogether. I'm sure they hoped that no one would remember who had invited them to come.

I set my things down beside the bench close to the backboard. As I unpacked my racket, I saw a few cars roll into the parking lot, music blaring. The police officer stood outside of her own, leaning on its hood. I positioned myself in front of the backboard and began to hit. Out of the corner of my eye, over the movement of my arm, I saw Keith hop from his car. He moved in strides towards the court with a ball in hand, speaking back to the others that followed him with a smile. They were hardly to the sidewalk when the police officer saw.

"Hey! Stop right there."

Slowly, without drawing too much attention, I stopped hitting and listened. I could not hear everything the officer said, but I understood the message. She kept her hand on her taser while speaking to the players. There were only three of them, all wearing red shirts with black athletic shorts. The hem of their clothes swayed with the breeze while they conducted their argument. I heard one mention a village that did not exist. The officer didn't check her device. She shook her head.

"No, you need to go," she told the players.

Keith slapped the ball. He looked all around, and then made eye contact with me. It was as though he believed I had some power over the situation, any more than he did. I held his gaze for a moment, then turned towards the backboard. I heard expletives as the players moved towards their cars.

I continued to hit. I was happy to be playing again. Some of the neighbors, who only days ago had yelled at me to go home, now smiled and waved at me when they passed. I smiled back.

***

The police officer left at the end of each day, so the players started showing up at night. My father often saw them as he returned from his delivery. He said that they were quieter than before, and fewer in number. My father laughed at the fact that no matter how many locks, passcodes, or *no trespassing* signs the neighborhood put in their path, the players found a way to play basketball. "Them boys love that sport," my father declared. I admired this as well.

The neighborhood association saw things differently. They posted a police officer in the parking lot at night. After a few days, the players stopped showing up once more. My father mentioned being followed through the neighborhood on his way home from work. My mother stopped going on her occasional evening stroll. I stopped venturing out too late after dark as well. The images on the news that summer discouraged any of us from trying our luck. We didn't want any trouble.

Some of the younger people in the neighborhood took issue with the heightened police presence. With everything else happening in our country, they seemed to make some connection between it all. Some spray-painted curse words in the parking lot beside the courts. Others threw toilet paper and empty bottles onto the sidelines. How they managed to do this without the officers arresting them is beyond me. But they managed.

***

The next time I went to hit against the backboard, there were two officers present, both men. One was bald and wore sunglasses, while the other had a full head of brown hair. The bald one looked to be around my father's age—maybe forty or fifty, while the other looked to be around mine. Neither had I ever seen before. They stopped me as was usual, but were not as polite as the woman before. The younger one held my arm while the other spoke.

"Name and address?"

I provided them with both. The officers spent extra time checking their devices while I held my tennis gear and waited. They seemed unimpressed with my diction and more concerned with my history. They asked me questions about my parents' names, the neighborhood, and other trivia. I answered all correctly. Finally, the one put away his device. The other said, "One hour limit on the basketball court."

"I'm here to play tennis," I replied. I held up my tennis racket for proof. The officers stared at me for a moment, reevaluating.

"Same rules apply."

I kept my practice short that day. Perhaps if I had known that would be the last time I ever used the courts, I would have stayed longer. The officers watched me hit the entire time. When a car drove by and the driver yelled, "Fuck you," and the younger officer yelled "Fuck you" back, I thought it would be safest to leave.

The last time I walked to the tennis court, I did not even reach the fence. It was poor timing that I arrived just as the officers made the arrest. It was the same two as the day before, and when the bald one looked at me over Keith's body, pressed tight against the hood of his car, I held my tennis racket up to show that I was only there to play, hoping he would remember. The officer stared at me, and when I backed away from him, he shouted, "Drop the weapon!"

"But I'm—

"Drop it!"

I laid my tennis racket on the ground and put my open hands in the air. My father taught me to do this, should a situation like this one ever occur. One of his dinner table lectures from years past. The bald officer turned to his coworker.

"Grab him, too."

By this point the neighbors began to gather around the recreation area. There were murmurs and gasps, and grins, and nods of affirmation as if to say, "I told you this would happen." There were cellphones and cameras held up as well. The younger officer made his way over to me, and as he put the handcuffs on, I kept my mouth shut and my body still. It was difficult not to resist as he jerked my arms behind me and shoved my legs forward. But as I watched Keith flounder like a fish against the bald officer's forceful arms, I knew what not to do. Even in my stillness, I couldn't help but let my eyes water.

"He lives here," one of the neighbors said. She pointed at me. "His parents live in this neighborhood. I'll take him home. He lives here."

The white woman moved towards me. She may have been one of my mother's friends. The officer and she walked away from his car, and there was a discussion about my fate that I could not hear. When the conversation ended, the officer walked back over, and handled my body with more care than before. He removed the handcuffs. When I turned and looked into his eyes, he gave me a worried smile and spoke slowly, as if I might not understand.

"Be real careful out there, bud," he said.

I wanted to ask about Keith, but I knew that he was on his own. As the officers drove away, I turned to see the woman who'd spoken on my behalf standing before me, perhaps to see if I was okay, or maybe waiting for thanks. I nodded my head towards her in acknowledgement. "Come on," she said, reaching out to me. She led me home.

***

JUSTICE FOR KEITH was what some of the signs read. Others read ACAB or some other variety of anti-cop rhetoric. The events in our neighborhood made the news. Teenagers and people my age, and older folks as well came from all over to stand on the sidewalk in the mid-summer heat and protest. My father brought them water bottles and Gatorades on days the sun sweltered. My mother wrote letters to the neighborhood association. Its leaders decided that the basketball courts should leave.

I did not attend any of the protests that summer. My protesting days were over. With no more recreation area to occupy my time, I found a job at a local tennis club, teaching white children the game many of their parents were surprised I knew. My father called it a "reparation hire" though my mother said I earned it. Some of my students were the children of our neighbors, who had apparently concluded tennis wasn't so bad. They talked to me about what a shame it was how everything went down, and how the neighbor's association should have predicted what would occur. "You build basketball courts, you're going to get basketball players," they said. Those could've been my father's words.

Coaching was not playing, and some days, I missed the game. But at the end of long shifts, I had little to no desire. One evening after work, I ignored my exhaustion. I drove into the city, into a park where there were courts. On them, I saw players who looked like me, serving, volleying, running, and smiling beside a basketball court full of trash talk and laughter. I waited for an hour, but there were no courts available. I drove home.

MOSES OJO

"Telephone"
Digital Art, 2020

The artwork talks about love life of a woman to her beloved husband after he went to fight for his country during the war. They talked all the time through the public telephone and shared love together like they were never apart.

REMI RECCHIA

Ninety Days

We're standing at the ocean, a used sea-
shell peering nervously through your beehive.
Sunday trash blinks up at us through sandy
exoskeletons and footprints. It will strangle the seagulls
when they touch down to feed. Maybe in the dawn.
   Maybe in the dark.
Maybe the crabs will have gone home by then, tucked
in their pincers and blue blood.

Is the seagull nocturnal? I can never remember—
some poet!—but I remember the joke well:

What do you get when you cross a bird with a sting ray?

Beloved, this beach would wash your face out
if you were but one freckle less lovely.
When I showed up late to our first
date, I should have dropped to my knees
in the middle of that parking lot, rested
mismatched shoes on bird shit and magicked
my way to an instant one-year sobriety chip.

In this mythos, I am golden clean before
we wed. In actual fact, I am ninety days sober
seven years after the first blackout avalanche, and your eyes
startle me in the shock of the sun.

What do you get when you cross an alcoholic with a train?

At the water's mouth, now, curled lip where the tectonic
motion sneaks toward our feet, I wonder
if you can hear my pulse. I cradle it in my swollen
coronary arteries, feel its echo in my bruised-for-two liver.
I wonder if you'll believe me when I say, yes,
my pupils have always been this large.

The Puddling

Nora watched from the safety of the surf shop as the tourists fled. Soon they packed in tightly beside her, the smell of sweat and damp towels nearly unbearable. Nora and Lucas had hoped if they waited out the storm, it would clear, yet the sky grew darker with each crack of thunder.

Four more beachgoers darted into the shop, and the group of soggy strangers lurched closer to the window. The air felt thin, and Nora's chest grew tighter; her mind flashed to a fatal crush at a soccer game.

"Any luck?" Nora turned to her husband who was refreshing his weather app.

"Storming for the next two hours," he said.

"I think we should make a run for it."

The boardwalk shops were only five blocks from their Airbnb bungalow, meaning it was a twelve-minute walk and faster if they booked it. So they ran, and ran, and ran, and the rain drenched them like they were nothing but specks of broken seashells. Nora and Lucas kept running, flip-flops drowned in rising puddles. Lucas was a few yards ahead of her, his t-shirt clinging to his back, his muscular calves sloshing through the growing river that was once Main Street, and she thought, *How I love this man.* She was buzzing like the sky. Nora hadn't felt this joyful—this exhilarated since before—

Something grabbed her ankle.

Nora's hands and knees slapped the asphalt.

"Lucas!" she cried.

He turned to her on all fours in a ten-inch puddle, and he doubled back.

"You okay?" He was yelling over the drilling rain.

All Nora could do was nod. She dared a glance behind her, yet there was nothing but water water everywhere. They had to get out of these puddles where Nora had felt five small fingers press into her ankle, felt the crescents of fingernails dig into her skin.

They ran the last block to the bungalow hand in hand.

***

Back at the house, Lucas grabbed towels as Nora sat in a patio chair inspecting her ankle. Five small bruises were already starting to form.

"Quite the digger you took out there," Lucas said, tossing her a striped towel.

"I didn't fall," Nora said. She knew as soon as she spoke it the day would shift, but the words bubbled up all the same. "Someone grabbed me."

"What?" Lucas didn't meet her gaze. "Let me get you some peroxide."

"Wait, please," she called him back. "Just look at this." She showed him the marks on her ankle. "Someone *grabbed* me."

Lucas lightly touched her leg, slanted his brow. "At the surf shop?"

"Are you listening? When I fell."

"You mean you were pushed?"

"No," Nora's stomach squeezed. "I mean—I don't know."

She had landed in less than a foot of water. If anyone had been lying there, she would have seen them. But she *had* felt a hand around her ankle, felt it pull her down, felt it only release its grip when Lucas approached.

Nora's frustration burned wet in the corners of her eyes. "It sounds weird, but I'm sure of it. I didn't trip—it was a hand."

"Nora," Lucas's cheeks slackened. "How could that happen?"

And then Nora's eyes went wide. "A sewer grate—I must have stepped on a sewer grate. Someone was down there and grabbed me."

"Like a clown?" he said with a smirk.

Nora's heart rose with the pitch of her voice. "Maybe someone fell down the sewer—maybe they were reaching for help." If someone was down there, they were in danger, probably drowning as all that water washed in from the storm. In the moment, she had panicked thinking it was a monster when she should have tried to help. "It felt like a small hand—it could have been a kid!"

"Okay, okay," Lucas said. Nora watched his face turn serious. "Let's go look then," he said, glancing out the window. "The rain's clearing."

They headed back down Main Street, this time, instead of the sky, their eyes were on the ground. Nora and Lucas inspected each sewer grate for signs of life, but every one they passed was just four slotted bars through which they could see to the bottom.

"It doesn't make sense," Nora said. "How can a person fit down there?"

"Probably built so a person *can't* fit down there, ya know?"

Nora turned to her husband, chest blazing. "So you don't believe me?"

Lucas looked at her kindly, took her hands in his. "You didn't *see* a kid or anything—you *felt* something. Maybe some seaweed got washed up from the drain, or a jellyfish or—"

"But I'm bruised," Nora said motioning to her ankle.

"You could have landed on something—"

Nora felt a familiar tension seize her chest. "Or maybe I'm just crazy?" she asked. She pushed his hands away.

Lucas appeared struck. "You know I don't think that."

After all her mood swings the last few years, after all the ways her unruly body heeded no one, did she know anything for sure?

"Then help me," she said, the edge in her voice gone. She looked down the road as the crowds returned. There was no time to waste. They'd have to call the beach police. Then the police would call a team to search the sewers, and Nora was sure as hell Lucas didn't want to have anything to do with that. Nora wanted to call him out on this, tell him his perfect beach trip wasn't worth a child's life; but now, a group of teens were skateboarding across Main Street; now, families were flip-flopping down the sidewalk carrying inflatable tubes and beach chairs. Now, as the sun peeked through the clouds, it was hard to believe a kid could be trapped inches below their feet. Her resolve was receding with the flood water. It was true she hadn't actually *seen* a child or even a hand, and now from her new angle, it seemed to Nora that maybe she'd been running in the middle of the road, not in reaching distance of the sewers at all.

"Maybe something did grab your leg," Lucas said, "but maybe it wasn't a kid drowning in the sewer. Maybe it isn't anything that needs our help."

She looked at her husband, his reassuring face masking his desperation to go back to sand, skee-ball, and strawberry ice cream, but really wanting to go back to last year. When life hadn't been so cruel to them.

"Okay," she said. She bit the inside of her cheek. "Let's forget it." And they headed back to the bungalow to grill hotdogs.

***

A week later, Nora and Lucas returned from the beach, falling back into their normal routine of work and home life. But Nora hadn't forgotten about the incident. Sometimes she'd think back to those fingers clasped around her ankle, then glance at her husband watching TV or cooking dinner and feel so monstrously lonely.

It was another ordeal that Nora shared alone.

That morning, Nora watched the summer rain pelt the window of her home office, but by her lunch break, the skies cleared, and she leashed up their dog for a walk. She and Fozzie headed down the driveway, puddles of water dotting the road. She felt her hair frizz in the spongy air as Fozzie's collar jingled like silver bells, and the whole neighborhood glistened as if given a power washing. Nora felt a surprising tickle of hopefulness.

It wasn't long before she stepped in one of the puddles, a puddle much deeper than she'd expected, felt the shock of water seeping through her sneaker, and when she drew it out, something—some*one* had hold of her ankle.

She screeched and pitched forward. Fozzie darted ahead. Again, her body crashed into the asphalt, but she didn't let go of the leash as Fozzie tugged her forward—as fingers—tiny strong fingers—gripped her shoe. With a sharp kick, she freed herself and jumped back to her feet.

Trembling, she peered into the puddle. A horrified face stared back, but it was only her own. She grabbed a stick and with a shaking hand, dipped it in the puddle, waited for a gremlin to grab its jagged edge. But nothing happened, and all she felt was the road.

She walked Fozzie home, giving a wide berth to any puddles. As soon as she got in the door, she reached for her phone to call Lucas at work. He'd be sitting in his office with his six co-workers, maybe even his boss. Of course, he'd try to rationalize it—*of course he wouldn't believe a monster was in a puddle.* Her lip quivered imagining his reassuring words that she already knew she'd interpret as condescending. Instead, she headed to the medicine cabinet and with shaking hands, typed the names of her prescriptions into her phone with the word "side effects."

The results flooded the screen.

Hot flashes. Mood swings. Headaches. Upset stomach. Weight gain.

All to be expected.

Drowsiness. Bloating. Pain at the injection site.

Nothing about hallucinations.

She found some posts on Reddit. Women stating that their medication gave them such severe anxiety and depression that they quit their jobs and still couldn't function properly years later. Nora's mouth went dry. Instead of stepping into a puddle, Nora was barreling down a dangerous rabbit hole, her eyes unblinking, tab after tab open, bookmarked. She shut off her screen and told herself to calm the fuck down.

But the next day when it was time for Fozzie's walk and drops battered the windows, Nora looked at her dog's brown bear eyes, brushed off her niggling guilt, and headed back to her home office. Fozzie whined at the door for an hour but eventually fell asleep on the couch he wasn't allowed on while Nora pretended not to notice.

When Lucas got home from work, Fozzie greeted him with wild joy.

"Whoa, buddy. You're all riled up." And then to Nora. "Did he get his walk today?"

"Work was too busy," she said, not meeting his eyes. "I'm thinking maybe we hire a dog walker as a backup."

***

But Nora couldn't escape the puddles.

Not after a downpour while grocery shopping speckled tide pools all over the parking lot. Not after a tropical storm off the coast left them with a sopping wet weekend and a river for a driveway. Not after the newly hired dog walker got the stomach bug and called out sick. Each walk, Nora bounded over puddles like she was navigating a gasoline leak, a sewage spill, a tide of lava. Every now and again, she'd feel a pull on her pant cuff, a fingernail on her ankle, but she was ready, she was fast, she pulled away, she kept up her deranged bunny hop.

"What's your deal?" Lucas finally asked after a few weeks of her bobbing around like a jack-in-the box. She had just leapt over a tiny puddle in their driveway as if hurdling in the 100-meter race.

She could tell him about the thing in the puddles. How they hadn't left it at the beach. How it kept reaching for her.

And then he could respond with some form of *You're over-stressed* or *It's all in your head.* She wouldn't blame him this time. It did seem crazy.

Then there was also the possibility he'd be really concerned.

He'd want to put their cycle on hold.

They'd just started trying to make a baby again, not the fun old-fashioned way, but the way with needles. Long ones, short ones, ones shaped like epi-pens, ones shaped like nightmares. So many needles she could imagine their baby born in the shape of one of those tomato pincushions from her grandmother's sewing box.

And through every ultrasound, every injection, every small success and failure, Lucas was there rubbing her back, icing her belly, cracking jokes to distract her as he stuck her again and again. He was a partner in every way. But in the end, it had been her body that had failed, her fertility that was "unexplained."

He was a partner by choice, but she was the one who felt each pinprick, she was the one getting poked with syringes and prodded with ultrasound wands, she was the one whose body needed to adapt to the medicine, to learn to have a baby, she was the one feeling things that couldn't be. So, when he asked her again if something was wrong, she responded, "I just don't want to get my shoes wet."

She heard Fozzie whining at the front door as she tucked herself into bed, claiming the medicine was making her drowsy.

It was 5 pm and she hadn't walked Fozzie in days.

***

Lucas knocked gently on the bedroom door.

"If you're going to nap," he said, "we should do the shots now, before we forget." He was holding a box filled with syringes. This was the routine every night before dinner: set the table, feed Fozzie, stick two needles in her belly.

Over one year ago, after four IVF cycles, after one embryo transfer, after ten more weeks of shots, there was one pregnant Nora. The last good memory she had before everything went to hell was when she felt the dripping between her legs, saw the fluid below her feet, yelled to Lucas that it was time though it was far too early.

The last time there was a puddle beneath her feet, she had sworn a baby would come out of it.

And now here she was, likely experiencing vivid delusions. She could see a psychiatrist who'd probably want to prescribe her some medication that couldn't mix with her current IVF protocol. The psychiatrist would recommend she pause the cycle, wait until she was feeling better. Wait until the delusions subsided. But after all this time and all these tries, Nora was certain that was no option.

Lucas handed her an alcohol swab to wipe down her belly as he prepared the needles on their dresser. While he filled each with medicine, he sang Marvin Gaye's "Let's Get It On" like he usually did to lighten the mood. Nora couldn't muster a smile. She clutched the fat of her belly and pressed a piece of ice to it, bracing herself for the pinch of the first needle.

"You're doing great, babe," Lucas said as he pierced her tender skin. She took a shallow breath as she felt the burn of the medicine crawl through her insides. He withdrew the needle and the tiniest smudge of red bloomed on her stomach.

"You okay?" he said, handing her a cotton ball. She nodded even though it still hurt.

As her husband prepared the second syringe, her mind sailed. She turned to him, blinking back tears. "Do you think Sam was the only chance we had?"

Sam was the little boy who had been growing inside of Nora. The one who had a lifetime of hopes and dreams attached to him before they'd even met him. He'd play the trumpet like his father, be good at math like his mother, maybe go to law school, volunteer at a non-profit, but then there was just a splash of amniotic fluid at her feet, and now Nora dreamed for him no more.

A genetic abnormality, the doctors had said. Next time, they'd pay thousands on extra tests—if there was a next time.

"No," Lucas said. "I don't think Sam was our only chance." He was now holding the bright red sharps container like an infant. "We're going to get a baby one way or the other." Lucas was thinking surrogacy, adoption, any of the alternative options thrown around when IVF complications seemed an insurmountable hurdle.

"Maybe…" her voice trailed off and her eyes turned away from him.

"You know I'm with you no matter what. We're a team."

But she barely heard him. All she could think about was that it was going to storm tomorrow.

***

The next morning, Nora and Fozzie watched the rain pelt the windows from the living room couch. She stroked his chocolate fur and wondered if she'd ever feel safe to walk him again, then wondered if she'd ever care for anyone other than her own dog. Could Fozzie's licks and nuzzles be enough love for a lifetime? Since last night's conversation, every time she looked at Lucas, a well of tears drowned her words. She was coming apart. Her old therapist's number was cued up on her phone, but instead she watched the rain accumulate in little swimming pools along her street.

If she wasn't going to get psych meds, then the only chance she had of ever leaving her couch would be to confront the fear—see it till its nearest end. What was that called? Exposure therapy? So what if the supposed puddle dweller grabbed her? She couldn't drown in a puddle, could she? Even if she could drown, couldn't the opposite happen, as well? Couldn't there actually be someone in the puddle, and couldn't she pull them out?

Couldn't it be a child?

The rain was now a roar, her phone blared the alarm for flash flooding, and Nora decided to go for a walk.

She put on her rain jacket, searched the bowels of the closet for her galoshes.

"What are you doing?" Lucas asked.

"Going for a walk."

"Nora—"

"You don't have to come," she said, pulling on her rubbers.

"Fozzie's not."

"You haven't wanted to walk in weeks," he said, his face growing more distraught. He flung a desperate hand to the window as lightning lit up the foyer. "And now you want to go?"

Lucas reached for her arm, but she batted it away. His face looked like a cracked mirror but what did it matter? She flung open the front door and took off.

"Nora!"

The rain was a chainsaw. Lucas screamed her name, but Nora ran. The street was already starting to flood. Her eyes searched and searched and then she found it. The widest, deepest one.

She stepped in—

Felt the cool water lap against her galoshes—

She stepped deeper and deeper into the puddle on the street—

The puddle that swaddled her like a knitted blanket until the rain and wind were just an echo. The puddle, the one that could bring her to Sam.

And this time, she'd reach back to him. She'd pull him up. Or he would pull her under. Either would do. Or maybe it wasn't him at all, but another baby. A new one. The one she was meant to have. The one she could birth into the world from this watery womb. She reached and she reached into the depth, waiting to feel the brush of fingertips.

And then a shadow cast upon her and her eyes turned up to the light.

Lucas.

He hovered above her, calling her name, eyes searching the puddle.

Fear gripped her, instead. Lucas would try to rescue her. He would drag her up, and all would be lost. He couldn't possibly understand. He couldn't possibly see.

Our baby, Nora willed him to know, *it's on its way.*

And then a splash, a flurry of bubbles.

A hand. But not a baby's hand.

One large and calloused and familiar. A hand that had rubbed her back, hugged her shoulders, brushed her cheek—this warm hand cradled her own.

Instead of pulling her out, Lucas had jumped in.

She held tighter, squeezed back, felt his silver ring click against her own.

And so they waited there together, floating in the inky black, for ten tiny fingers to greet their own.

LYNNE SCHMIDT

When it happens, you let it happen

My aunt gave me this command
asked "Can you handle this?"

I lied and told her yes,
and pulled up a chair,

and watched my babcia breathe
in and out and in and out and in.

My aunt came back,
and we sat for hours.

My partner brought food,
and we sat vigil, pausing at times,

to see if the breathing had stopped.
Years later, I sit alone at her bedside.

The ceremony is the same, but substantially different.
Previously she would be the one to foresight,

"It will be eight hours"
And now, it is me telling me mother,

"She won't last until tomorrow."
Wrapped in plastic, I hold her fever.

I chant meditations to her,
"you have nothing else to do,

Nowhere else to be,
Just right here,

Right now."
I tell her I get it now,

Why she sent me away before because I wasn't ready then.
I tell her I am now.

I promise, I can handle it.
If and only if so this way, she does not die alone.

And as her breathing accelerates,
I grab her hand one final time.

I tell her loud enough any God within earshot can hear,
"I love you"

And she exhales
and her body

lets go.

PHIL TEMPLES

"Egress"

Color Photograph Shot at 7 Gloucester Street, Boston, MA, Modified with
B&W Filtering, 2/27/2021

I've always been attracted to mobile photography in urban areas.
I'm partial to back alleys, fire escapes, graffiti-strewn walls or
store fronts. Nature shots of majestic sunsets or mountain rang-
es just aren't very satisfying to me. I shoot using a smartphone
in auto mode—a Samsung Galaxy S10e. I'm too lazy to carry
around my sophisticated Canon EOS 5D because it's bulky and
weighs a ton. If I did, I'm certain that I would end up missing
all kinds of shots while fiddling with the controls. While rush-
ing to a doctor's appointment early one morning, I was fortunate
to glance down a Boston alleyway. I was able to catch the sun
reflecting at just the right angle to create a wonderful scene.

Fold the Shadows

Yes, at first, I tried brevity,
used contractions, looked
for substitutions of formal

constructions. *Won't* replaced
maybe after the night a stranger
split me, when I curled small

in my Honda. Words like *shouldn't*
squatted, & I refused to abandon
them. Years passed. On a mission,

I truncated my expressions—
I added *can't* & *didn't* to *won't*.
My shortcomings added up;

they elongated my mother's
drawling disapproval. No one
listened. A witchy chorus

of skeptics hovered on broomsticks.
Why should someone believe
me, anyway? Midnight tonight

in a desolate meadow. In the distance,
orange groves burn. I study moths
with fellow lepidopterists. A kid

asks, *What gives us value? Is it breath?
Or goodwill?* He watches me tend
to a grey insect struggling

in the confines of its thin net,
scrapping through the early
morning flashlight penumbras,

tugged toward death. Oh, the magnetism
of demise—it's irresistible tonight.
Those long-leaf pines slash their own

shadows. Yet still, I battle elisions
that lurk in gravitas, & I employ
diction no one gets. Words

like *victim* transcend this page turn's
tectonics. I still possess power,
but I'm diminished to bulges & bad

knees. I can summon a summer
night from memory, weave spells
that hearken back to the evil taste

of a .45 on my tongue. I conjure
ruin out of *nothing* when *nothing* pleats
spectral places, those ensorcelled

hours when slavering devils howl
toward morning. With my old-fangled
magic, *I'm* self-destructs to *I am*

not. Chilling verbs act & wink
& flirt & force & command.
They slide over from the passenger

seat, & the phantom of my rapist
uncrimps. There's no trick to forgetting
terror, to losing that midnight,

that time I lay prone on my vinyl
backseat, inhaling my attacker's
four-day-old scent. The shortest

complete sentence in the English
language never chases away
the horror or my mother's shame.

No.

How To Use Your Father's Lawn Mower

TROY-BILT®
Owner's Manual
Fire-Red Push Lawn Mower
Model #Not-Sure-But-Don't-Care

REVIEW INSTRUCTIONS CAREFULLY AND DIFFUSE SPARKS OF ANGER BEFORE ATTEMPTING USE OF MACHINE.

WARRANTY

This mower has been well maintained by its owner since the date of purchase years ago. Now that its owner has left, it is required that you, the eldest daughter, take over its use and restore decency to the yard. Do this for your mother, who is swamped by mediation meetings. For your younger sisters, who are still processing the shock.

For the HOA, who recently mailed a warning about the height of the grass.

SAFETY RULES

IMPORTANT: Improper use of mower could result in thrown objects, severed limbs, or worse.

Attempted use may result in feelings of stupidity. After all, you are seventeen years old and should know how to mow a lawn.

General use *will* result in the feeling that your family's collective ego has been damaged. Neighbors in your tight, suburban cul-de-sac will see you fumbling in the blistering June heat and wonder why your father is missing from the landscape he always tended so faithfully. They didn't know about the situation, he always smiling and she always trying to, muffled cries lingering on the other side of your bedroom wall. They didn't know, but you did.

Swallow hard, then swallow hard again.

ASSEMBLY

Free the mower from its hibernation in the cluttered garage and wheel it toward the front lawn. Hesitation may linger; the front lawn was always closely guarded, a sacred exhibit of neatly trimmed grass. Pleas to do *just one cartwheel* were met with *you have an entire backyard to play in.* Failure to comply, even by the accidental veering of your scooter off the sidewalk, resulted in heart-pounding reproofs.

But all of that is absent now. The exhibit's curator just moved into a gated apartment complex across town. He recently tried to make you feel at home there.

Do you want to go out and see the pool?

No, Dad. I don't want to see the pool.

OPERATION

It is advised that you familiarize yourself with the location of
various controls and adjustments before operation. It is advised
that you raise the mower blades to better accommodate grass left
untouched since the afternoon your aunt whisked you and your
sisters to Panera while your father packed.

Since your energy is waning, focus on the essentials—namely,
starting the engine.

Repeat, once more, the instructions your mother gave you
while she sifted crinkled court documents: *Pull the handle to the
thing, then yank the cord.* Angle your body in different ways to
better clutch the "handle" and the "thing," which protrude to a
height that makes your five-foot-one-inch frame feel incapable of
generating any steering force.

Now, yank the cord. No, *Yank!* Invest all the exclamation
points you can muster. Attempt three, four, five times. More, if
necessary.

And, with a jerk and a roar, plunge forth.

Push, arms straight out, into the chaos of a new world. Awk-
wardly blaze each crooked row. Wince but endure the exploding
grass stinging your bare legs, the stench of gasoline filling your
nostrils.

Trample your way across the old exhibit, digging your heels in
as you leave a disarray of razed shoots. Curve around the right
and left flanks of the house, side-eyeing the obliviously joyful
hydrangea bushes running along the vinyl siding.

Conquer the sloping backyard, repressing those sudden
memories of laughter and fresh air. Clip, as best as possible,
the irregular tufts of grass jutting around the playground set he
built, sweating over wooden slats while you slurped homemade
popsicles. Pause at the base of the wide patio deck, the location

of countless family get-togethers, where he would grill pizza and pump Afro-Latin music through the outdoor speakers.

STORAGE

When all is finished—the echo of the engine still battering your eardrums—stop and look.

Look at yourself, at your drenched T-shirt, your sore arms, your chlorophyll-stained sneakers. Look at the grass, the rows uneven yet subdued in the afternoon sun. You don't have to pretend to feel pleased. But at least acknowledge your accomplishment.

Save this manual for future reference. For when your father starts a new life halfway across the country. For when the needs left behind become more serious than that of an unruly suburban yard. It's not a small task, learning how to live like this.

But you will learn.

YVANNA VIEN TICA

Saudade Accuses Brown Girl

We were children or maybe
you were & I was just trapped

in the belief of one. Even now
every memory is tinged with moonlight.

No one believes me when I say
you were a natural blonde as if a nocturnal couldn't

approach the light without bleeding. Did you notice
how invisible we were to the trains that passed

our suburb with nowhere to go.
Or maybe they did have plans & I was just

preoccupied in wishing to leave like a rapture.
No one believes me when I say I couldn't have

done better. As if a moon could
hide under my fingertips without leaking

all over you. As if a gentle rage could
make you change your mind. We were children after all

or maybe that was how you justified it, invisible even
to yourself. Could you stand it, loving an accented tongue,

a brown skin. I always did smell different
from the white girls, all green mangoes and spices

where the subtle notes of Bath & Body fruit mist
should have been. Where the forced laughter should have
been. You hated it

when I was honest about your terrible
jokes. No one believes me when I say you stole

all your pick-up lines from Reddit threads or maybe
you lied to me about that too. Could you

stand it, your parents' questions after I left
the family dinner. You never could muster the courage

or maybe I am just wishing to see things differently.
As if a moon could ever lick its own

milk skin. Even now every memory stings bitter
like the unexpected aftertaste of green mangoes flushed with salt.

KIM ELLINGSON

Holiday Party 2017

You might have been standing on the beach
in Silver Lake with your soon-to-be-ex-lover
while I numbed myself in the ancient
basement of the bar where I worked

on Old World Third Street—doing lines,
downing a bottle of red wine with an elephant
on the label, dipping my licked finger into a baggie
of crystalline molly as alcoholic rats chewed taps

of Spotted Cow. As you considered a move
to the Pacific Coast, a last-ditch effort
for you two, I lived in an East Side January,
considering only my own mouth,

how my teeth chattered themselves back to life
during an endless comedown from key bumps
in the bathroom, cab rides in pre-dawn blackness,
biting walks in lake effect wind.

CAROLYN GUINZIO

"Blankness Was Beauty"
Digital photo-collage, 2021

I am primarily a poet, and my work has always been deeply in-
volved with place and the idea of permanence. This piece is from
a sequence called LEAF. Meant to echo lacunae, LEAF is a series
of visual and text pieces consisting of macro-photos of disinte-
grating leaves, layered with handwritten text visible only through
the holes in the leaves. The illegibility is meant to acknowledge
the challenge of endeavoring to make something lasting. Even
if much of what we do sinks back into the earth, traces remain.
That the text requires magnification in print or radical zooming-
in on a screen is reflective of my desire for a sense of intimacy
between viewer/reader, to mitigate the coldness of digitally-
created work. A reader, holding the leaves (pages) in their hand,
will, I hope, feel as if they are holding the leaves (leaves) in their
hand.

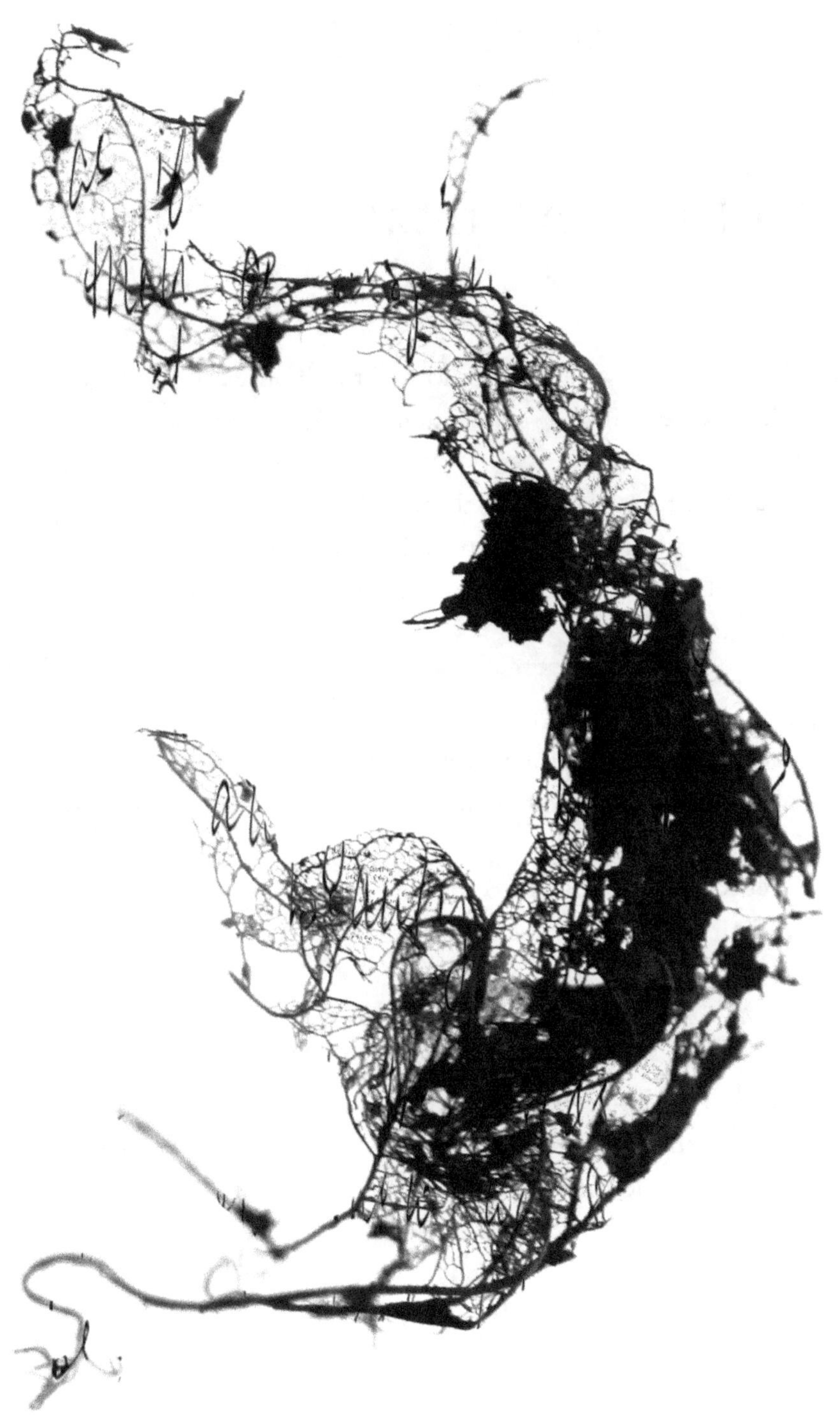

STEPHANIE STAAB

Il Lupo Mannaro

Even if I was asleep, I could feel that you were awake at night
like a werewolf   pacing a mountain pass.

We were foreigners to each other.
The language you spoke to tell me something Important
was different than the language you spoke in bed, your mother
tongue.

I have, of course, a recording of your voice
the same ten questions I asked everyone.
You couldn't remember the story of how your parents met.

I let my mother listen to that interview once
and although she is a church lady
she said *Wow*
you two must have had great sex after that…

Signs came and went:
an ill-wish placed above our door by a jealous ex-lover
unquenchable thirsts
fangs.

Then, you set out for the woods
and I never saw you again.

Sometimes when I'm not expecting anyone and the doorbell
rings
I still think it's going to be you
darkening the doorway
no suitcase, no coat, just you
translated.

I wonder if sometimes you pause to take a sip of water
on the trail towards Jungfrau
if you kick the snow
and remember how you used to wake me up
from under the covers, hours after midnight
to kiss me or hold me.

The dream of the Alpinist.

Dalí

I met Dalí in my husband's architecture studio, which was the detached one-car garage behind our house. My husband said Dalí had started coming by in the afternoons and critiquing his work.

"Dalí? As in Salvador Dalí?" I said, pulling reheated enchiladas from the oven. "I thought he was dead."

"Well, he certainly has a lot of opinions for a dead guy," my husband said, plopping dollops of guacamole on his plate, leaving a smear in the bowl for me to scrape out with my finger.

***

I had been sitting at my desk all morning, bouncing between a blank screen where a future best-selling romance should be and a motivational article touting the benefits of self-talk. It said studies had shown that pro athletes who spoke out loud to themselves in the third person were more successful than those who used first-person I statements.

I toggled back to my blank screen.

"Come on, Vivian. You can do this," I said out loud. *That is second-person*, I thought in silent rebuke. I tried again.

"Vivian can do this. Vivian is a winner. Vivian is the acclaimed author of the *Dusky Mangrove* pirate trilogy." I was basically reading the bio off the back of my last book. It was printed next to a black and white headshot of me in my mid-twenties with airbrushed cheekbones and the intense gaze of an emerging writer staring into a bright literary future. I wondered if that girl was seeing a middle-aged woman in enchilada-stained sweatpants, talking to herself in the third person, trying to replicate the alchemy of early success.

***

I walked in through the side door without knocking. The garage door was open, providing a panoramic view of the crumbling alley behind our house. My husband was hunched over his underlit drafting table. Dalí was on our ancient treadmill, jogging at a leisurely clip.

"Well, hello!" Dalí said with long, singsong vowels and languid, liquid Ls. He was wearing suede wingtips and had a wide, loping stride, as if he was fashionably floating from one moon crater to the next. The pointed ends of his moustache rebounded skyward with every step. He swept his arm grandly at the alleyway. "A most inspiring vista for a stroll going nowhere!"

A rat skittered past.

My husband had moved back to his desk, head swallowed behind a massive monitor. "He is inspired as well," Dalí said.

"I can see that."

"Are you, my dear?" Dalí asked.

I deflated onto the corrugated cardboard loveseat my husband designed when he was in college.

My husband's phone rang. He stood up and glared at the noisy treadmill. "Ken Law speaking." He plugged his finger into his ear and turned around.

Dalí stage-whispered to me behind the back of his hand, "It could be a very important client," stretching the length of his face in exaggerated awe. "We must let the master work in peace."

With that, Dalí gave me a courtly bow before leaping off the treadmill. He bounded out through the open garage door and disappeared down the alley, hurtling over cracked asphalt and detritus in his path.

My husband was still on the phone, his calm, professional voice swallowed by the noise of the running belt that echoed through the exposed rafters of our garage. I turned off the treadmill and quietly went back inside the house. I sat down at my computer to write but ended up spending the afternoon rereading a short story I had written years ago. It was about a woman who grows a tumor so large, it becomes another person entirely. The tumor eventually kills her and assumes her place in society, and her friends and co-workers are left none the wiser.

My agent at the time said this type of work was not for my market. It had no erotica, no swashbuckling, not even a whisper of illicit longing or intrigue.

***

Sometimes Dalí would come with Babou, an ocelot that liked to chew the tips of my fingers. "How can you stare at your keyboard all day but be so careless with your manicure?" Dalí would ask.

I told him I'm not looking at my hands, I am looking at the screen.

"Why bother looking at the screen when you say it is always blank?"

My husband never told me when Dalí was in his studio, and I never asked. There were many weeks he wasn't. When that was the case, I would nonchalantly say hello to my husband, feign interest in whatever he was working on, and then duck out when the explanation inevitably became too technical.

The unfinished drywall on the garage was covered with pinned renderings of a tall structure with pretty rectangular gables and lacy eaves. "They're for the competition I told you about—to build a new library in Persistence, Iowa," my husband said. "My design made it to the final round. Now, residents get to vote on the winning bid."

I peered at the colorful exterior. "Are those bricks all different colors?"

"My design is called *The Pixelization of Needlepoint*," my husband said.

The intricate design reminded me of love notes my husband wrote to me the first year we met. They were all on graph paper, one letter per box. I loved the look of them, the symmetry of the page, the precision of his all-capitalized penmanship, slanted just so. Of course, the prose was horrendous. But still, the letters were very sweet, complimentary, courtly and almost shy. While not a particular fan of romance novels, he wrote of his great admiration for my modest literary achievements. To him, I was an example of the linear trajectory of success that upper middle-class American youth is indoctrinated into. At the time, my husband was a draftsman for a prestigious firm whose titular architect contributed in name only. During my husband's tenure, the only thing he worked on was doors. In fact, the same door. Over and over again. On a rotating team with at least five other people, all quibbling over one single door. By the time this door was hung on a series of luxury villas in Florida, my husband had finally left the company to find fulfillment in our unfinished garage.

A few times I walked in on Dalí and my husband in conversation, but it was never about art or process. It was usually about sports, esoteric ones like cricket or curling. Or cage fighting.

"That's disgusting," I said.

"Do you not see the beauty of a bruise that blooms in front of your very eyes? It is painted with the most exquisite palette found in nature, the abject stain of man's irrepressible need to eviscerate Man," Dalí said. "The only time it is acceptable to celebrate the absolute annihilation of another human being is when thousands of people are watching, and money is on the line."

***

"One time I was in Burgundy. It was the very end of spring, and the sunflower fields were burning coronas into my retinae like all impertinent flowers do. We were there, of course, for the wine. But before my glass was poured, the purveyor of the vineyard, a simple French farmer, said, 'You must first eat this.' He went away to the kitchen and came back carrying a butcher block by its fat handle. He set it down in front of me. On it was the largest strawberry I had ever seen, as big as the heart of a sacred cow. It was deepest red, and the leaves were as green as a jealous rage. The stem was the thickness of my middle finger, and longer still. The strawberry was so enormous, I ate it with a steak knife. And when I cut into it, I swear to you, it bled. And inside this strawberry, once you were through the juicy red flesh, were the icy white chambers, so sweet, and so crisp, and so cold it made me shiver. Or maybe I was just shaking in ecstasy. I can't remember now. But I do remember it took me exactly twenty-seven minutes to eat the whole thing. And when it was done, I wept. Because it was done, and no one would ever know the pleasure. But, no, I didn't cry for anyone else. I cried for myself, because I knew I could not lose this virginity twice."

His eyes were closed, and his mouth was wet under his moustache. He smelled the air, conjuring the memory.

"Why did you tell me that?" I asked.

Dalí opened his eyes, appalled I would insert myself into a memory of such sensuous intimacy. "Because when I soliloquize, I don't have to suffer your banal conversation."

My eyes and throat went dry. I looked to my husband to have him reassure me that I am a sparkling wit, astute and uncanny. But he was so deeply immersed in the page under his pencil, I thought it best to leave him be. And besides, I would probably find his answer less than reassuring.

***

It was Dalí who told me the good news.

"The maestro! The creator!" Dalí said, bowing with flourish towards my husband. Dalí and his ocelot danced circles around the garage like lights shooting off a disco ball. My husband came over to me, his arms spread for a congratulatory hug, heart open for a word about how proud, how happy I was for him, for us.

"Now what?" I asked.

"I have to build a 3D model and go out to Persistence to do a site study. I'd also like to thank the town council in person," my husband said.

Dalí pointed to all the printouts taped to the wall. "Iowa is the Barcelona of the western world! The gentlepeople of Persistence understand symbol. They understand icon. Like Chinese characters, each a piece of art itself, the sum of their parts being more than mere text—it is a masterpiece!"

I looked more closely at the sketches of the building my husband was going to build. It was simultaneously quaint and edgy, modern and timeless, understated and ornate. It was perfect.

***

I texted my husband a poem I wrote while he sat next to me in bed, finishing his nightly crossword puzzle.

"What's this?" he said.

"It's an emoji haiku."

He gave it all of four seconds. "I don't get it," he said.

"It's representative iconography. Emoji as alphabet."

"But how is this a haiku? Isn't there supposed to be a certain number of syllables per line?"

"It's not about syllable count!" I said.

"Then is it hieroglyphics? Or, I don't know, emoji algebra?"

I wanted to scream.

My husband sighed. "Well, at least you're writing again."

"What's that supposed to mean?" I asked. "I write all the time."

"When? You spend all day in my office talking to Dalí."

"Why can you spend all day talking to Dalí and I can't?"

"Well, he's coming to my office, for one thing. He's not visiting yours."

I pulled the blanket to my chin, headbutted my pillow, and rolled away from my husband's brutality.

My husband sighed, reached over, and turned off the light. I lay in the dark, trying to channel my anger into words, into plot. I tucked myself into the deepest wrinkles of my brain, furiously looking for any sort of new story to tell, but eventually I faded into sleep, unable to find a single one.

***

The little model of the library took up a lot of room.

My husband stood over the drafting table with a pair of tweezers. Foam board, X-Acto knives, paint and all manner of adhesive were strewn on the ground and on every available surface in the garage. Dalí was sitting at my husband's computer, Googling himself. I was lounging on the cardboard sofa, trying to entice Babou away from my husband's delicate operation with a bowl of strawberries.

My husband frequently looked up, raking his hair, jaw clenched, sucking in air through nostrils flared like those on a rampaging horse. I didn't know what my husband was upset about. We were being very quiet, especially since we agreed that the treadmill would remain off while my husband was working. Still, my husband said, "Now that I have the library contract, I really think I need to find a legitimate office space. It would be nice to have a place to meet clients and just have room to spread out." He looked at me, as if I were the clutter.

"Excellent idea, my friend!" Dalí jumped up. "A redwood cannot reach the heavens if planted in a decrepit garage. Excitement awaits! Where shall we go?"

"We? You're not moving with him, are you?" My yelp was so high-pitched, the ocelot hissed.

"I go where I go," Dalí said breezily. Then he gestured to my husband. "To the redwoods! To the sky!"

I shuddered like a dead leaf right before it falls off the tree.

***

My husband had left to finalize paperwork for a raw office space downtown; Dali announced he was spending these last precious moments alone in the hallowed birthplace of brilliance itself. I found him sitting cross-legged on the bare cement floor. The garage door was closed, and the room was dim under the fluorescent bulb that flickered a sterile, bluish hue.

Dalí's eyes were closed and he was holding the end of a chain leash that was wrapped around Babou's neck. The ocelot was prancing on the treadmill, long claws shredding the belt with every step.

I could not tell if Dalí was asleep or meditating. I clinked the wine glasses I was carrying together. Dalí opened his eyes.

"For god's sake, put your breast back inside your shirt, ma'am," Dalí said.

I let my unbuttoned linen shirt slip further down my bare shoulders, long hem grazing the tops of my naked legs.

The bottle of wine I had brought was old and expensive, something my husband and I were saving for a celebratory occasion, say, a manuscript being sold or our fifteenth anniversary. I blew a fine layer of dust off the faded label.

Dalí was unimpressed. "What is this display before me?"

"Relax. Lie down," I said, trying to sound breathy, self-assured. "Please. Don't get up."

"I dine at the table of genius," Dalí said. "There is no reservation for me here." Dalí picked Babou up off the treadmill.

"Don't go! I need you!" I thrust myself forward, trying to grab Babou's leash and block the door. My bosom heaved like one of my romantic heroines, but the scene was not unfolding as I had written it. At this point I should have been smearing caviar on my inner thigh before being thrown onto Babou's back and riding away with Dalí to a world where elephants float on spindly legs and inspiration is evergreen.

Instead, Dalí stood mute before me, eyes dilated into saucers of horror and contempt. I could see myself in their oily reflection, a desperate, lazy, hateful woman. His silence, his imperious pity, I could not take.

I threw a wine glass, right at Dalí's head. It exploded against the back of the garage door in a spray of diamonds. Dalí closed his eyes and yawned. I threw the other one. It shattered on the ground in front of him. He didn't even flinch.

"I thought you said violence was disgusting," Dalí said drolly, picking up a shard of glass with the tips of his long fingers, sniffing it, then tossing it over his shoulder.

The heavy wine bottle was all I had left in my hands, but it was too heavy to throw. So I wielded it like a club over my head. Down it came, right onto the roof of the Persistence library.

The gables crumpled with pitiful ease. The bottle didn't even chip. I smashed it down again. And again. And again. I imagined all the little townspeople of Persistence huddled inside their stupid pixelized library, children sitting cross-legged during story time in the book nook, old women sewing cheery aphorisms onto ugly throw pillows in the community room. Each soul crushed, a particle of my husband's self-worth. I blighted them all until there was nothing left, until finally, finally the dark bottle cracked. Red wine rained over the collapsed pile of colored bricks, sanguine rivers spilling over the edge.

When I was finished, the treadmill was turned off, and Dalí and Babou were gone.

Red liquid streamed down my forearm. I licked my hand. It tasted like metal and vinegar, and not particularly expensive at all.

***

My husband is in Persistence, Iowa, building his dream. I listen to his voicemail greeting at least ten times a day. He sounds professional, friendly, distant. I hang up before the beep every time.

I have set myself up nicely in my new office. The treadmill is still here, and the floor is stained with motor oil and, now, wine. The cold hardness suits me and what I am writing. It is a novel, an expansion of my short story about the woman who grows a tumor. But now, instead of killing her, the tumor becomes a glittering, effervescent bon vivant; a living and loving organism that eats her tissue but feeds her creative soul.

CONTRIBUTORS

Sara Siddiqui Chansarkar is an Indian American writer. Born to a middle-class family in India, she later migrated to the USA with her husband and son. She currently lives in the suburbs of Ohio. She is a technologist by profession and a writer by passion. Her stories and poems have appeared in numerous publications, print and online. Her work has been selected for *Best Small Fictions 2022*. She won first place in ELJ Micro Creative Non-Fiction Prize, placed in the Strands International Flash Fiction Festival, and is the runner-up for the *Chestnut Review* Chapbook Contest. Her stories have been shortlisted in the Bath Flash Fiction Awards and *SmokeLong* Micro Competition. She is currently a Prose Editor at *Janus Literary* and a Submissions Editor at *SmokeLong Quarterly*. Her debut flash fiction collection *Morsels of Purple* was released in 2021. More at https://saraspunyfingers.com. Reach her @PunyFingers.

Carlos Contreras (they/them) is non-binary, Guatemalan, and working on a way to make it out of Texas. They are the lead fiction editor of *Alien Magazine*, and their recent publications can be found in *Complete Sentence*, *The Lumiere Review*, and *Passages North*. They also exist on Twitter @cafaco_.

William C. Crawford is a prolific itinerant photographer based in Winston Salem, NC. He travels the United States searching for slivers of Americana to elevate to eye candy. Please see Instagram @ bcraw44 for more of his work.

Kim Ellingson holds an MFA from Antioch University, and her poetry has appeared or is forthcoming in *Cagibi, Rejected Lit, Lost Balloon,* and elsewhere. She lives in Milwaukee and can be found on Instagram @its_a_lemon_tree.

Gabriela Gonzales is a writer from Nashville, Tennessee who writes about the strangely beautiful tragedy that is human connection. She has had work featured in *Awakened Voices Literary Magazine, Cosmonauts Avenue, Lost Balloon, Wigleaf,* and other journals. She really appreciates giraffes, the oxford comma, and babies dressed like hipsters.

Carolyn Guinzio is the author of seven collections, most recently *A Vertigo Book* (The Word Works, 2021), winner of the Tenth Gate Prize and current finalist for the Foreword Indies Award. Her work has appeared in *The New Yorker*, *The Nation*, *Poetry*, and many other journals. Among her previous books are *Spoke & Dark* (Red Hen, 2012), winner of the To The Lighthouse/A Room Of Her Own Prize and the visual poems *Ozark Crows* (Spuyten-Duyvil, 2018). Her website is carolynguinzio.tumblr.com.

Mattea Heller is a high school English teacher and has an MFA in Creative Writing from Western Connecticut State University. Her work appears in several literary magazines, the horror podcast *Thirteen*, and an upcoming episode of the podcast *Creepy*. You can find her at matteaheller.com.

Michelle Hulan (she/her) is a poet and writer whose work has appeared or is forthcoming in *Poet Lore*, *Mud Season Review*, and elsewhere. She is a graduate of the University of Ottawa's MA in English program and a Tin House Writer's Workshop alum. She lives in Brooklyn with her partner, child, and Pomeranian. Follow her on Twitter @ michellehulan.

Cate McGowan is an essayist, poet, fiction writer, and author of two books—she won the Moon City Press Short Fiction Award for her debut short story collection, *True Places Never Are*; her debut novel, *These Lowly Objects*, released in 2020. McGowan's work appears or is forthcoming in numerous literary outlets, including Norton's anthology *Flash Fiction International*, *Glimmer Train*, *The Citron Review*, *Shenandoah*, and *Tahoma Literary Review*. Find out more about Cate McGowan at https://catemcgowan.com.

Sue Mell is a writer from Queens, NY. She earned her MFA from Warren Wilson, and was a 2020 BookEnds fellow at SUNY Stony Brook. Her debut novel, *Provenance*, won Madville Publishing's 2021 Blue Moon Novel Contest and comes out in July 2022. Her collection of micro essays, *Giving Care*, won the 2022 Chestnut Review Prose Chapbook Prize, and her collection of short stories, *A New Day*, was a finalist for the 2021 St. Lawrence Book Award. Other work has appeared in *Cleaver Magazine*, *Hippocampus Magazine*, *Jellyfish Review*, *Narrative Magazine* and elsewhere. Find her at www.suemellwrites.com.

Moses Ojo is a young Nigerian art enthusiast who uses his mind as a Vista for making captivating arts while using his brushes and watercolors thereby speaking reality through his arts and crafts to his viewers.

Yasmin Nadiyah Phillip is a writer, musician, and freelance illustrator and photographer. She is currently based in northwestern Virginia.

Oormila Vijayakrishnan Prahlad is a Sydney artist, poet, and pianist of Indian heritage. She holds a Masters in English and is a member of the North Shore Poetry Project, and *Authora Australis*. She has been painting and exhibiting for the past twenty years and her paintings can be found in many private collections. She has been widely published in both print and online literary journals and anthologies, and her recent works have been showcased in *Dwell Time*, *Star 82 Review*, *Otoliths*, *3 AM Magazine*, and are forthcoming in *Club Plum Journal*, *Parentheses Journal*, *Pithead Chapel*, and elsewhere.

Remi Recchia is a trans poet and essayist from Kalamazoo, Michigan. He is a Ph.D. candidate in English-Creative Writing at Oklahoma State University. He currently serves as an associate editor for the *Cimarron Review* and Reviews Editor for *Gasher Journal*. A four-time Pushcart Prize nominee, Remi's work has appeared or will soon appear in *World Literature Today*, *Best New Poets 2021*, *Columbia Online Journal*, *Harpur Palate*, and *Juked*, among others. He holds an MFA in poetry from Bowling Green State University. Remi is the author of *Quicksand/Stargazing* (Cooper Dillon Books, 2021); his chapbook, *Sober*, is forthcoming with Red Bird Chapbooks in 2022.

Lynne Schmidt is the grandchild of a Holocaust survivor. They were a semi-finalist for the 2022 Button Poetry Chapbook Contest, and the winner of the 2021 The Poetry Question Chapbook Contest, and

2020 New Women's Voices Contest. Lynne is the author of the chapbooks, *SexyTime* (TPQ 2022), *Dead Dog Poems* (Finishing Line Press, 2021), *Gravity* (Nightingale and Sparrow Press, 2019), and *On Becoming a Role Model* (Thirty West, 2020). In 2012 they started the project, AbortionChat, which aims to lessen the stigma around abortion. When given the choice, Lynne prefers the company of her pack of dogs and one cat to humans.

Stephanie Staab is an American poet and translator living in the Black Forest. Her work has appeared in *Crab Creek Review, Ligeia Magazine, Summerset Review* and others. Her first chapbook, *Earthling*, is available now from Selcouth Station Press.

Renée Jessica Tan's work has appeared in *Flash Fiction Online, Everyday Fiction*, and *MacQueen's Quinterly*. Upcoming publications include *Gingerbread House* and *Wigleaf*. Her short story "Baghead" was featured on the *Selected Shorts* podcast that first aired October 2020. Her flash fiction story "Auntie Cheeks" was included in *Best Small Fictions 2021*. Renée lives with her first husband and two cats.

Phil Temples is a product of the Midwest but he currently lives in Watertown, Massachusetts. He likes to dabble in mobile photography. He's published several mystery-thriller novels, a novella, and two short story anthology in addition to over 180 short stories. You can learn more about Phil at https://temples.com.

Yvanna Vien Tica is a Filipina writer with a hearing impairment who grew up in Manila and a suburb near Chicago. Her poetry has appeared or is forthcoming in *Verse Daily, Poet Lore, Shenandoah, Poetry Northwest, The Rumpus*, and *Salt Hill*, among others. She reads for *Muzzle Magazine*, tweets @yvannavien, and will attend Yale University in the fall. In her spare time, she can be found enjoying nature and thanking God for another day.

Patrick van Raalten is a multidisciplinary artist. He is best described as an artistic adventurer. He loves photography and uses a PC and tablet to create a unique style of layered paintings and images. He is also an electronic music maker. He loves creating textile art, especially through weaving. In his life the creative and spiritual are interwoven. The Art of Life itself is the rich source from which his creativity and works arise. Central themes in his work are revelation, contemplation and the synthesis of form and emptiness.

Sasha Wade is a recent graduate of Bennington College MFA Writing Seminars and an attendee of The Bread Loaf Writers' Conference. She is currently working on her first book of poems, a portion of which will include several experimental translations of her great-grandfather, Alirio Diaz Guerra, poetry. Diaz Guerra was a prolific poet who was born in Colombia and later exiled to Brooklyn in 1895. Sasha's poetry has appeared in *Rust + Moth*, *The James Dickey Review*, *Third Wednesday*, *Front Porch Review*, and *The American Journal of Poetry*.

Joel Worford is a writer from Richmond, Virginia. His work appears/ is forthcoming in *trampset*, *The Lumiere Review*, *The Laurel Review* and more. Joel is the 2018 recipient of Longwood University's Outstanding Creative Writing Student Book Award. He received a Best of the Net nomination in 2019 for his short story "The Warning Sign," as well as a Pushcart nomination in 2021. Joel serves as Fiction Editor at *K'in Literary Journal*.

Chestnut Review

VOLUME 4 NUMBER 2 AUTUMN 2022

FOR STUBBORN ARTISTS

COVER ART

Kelly Sargent
"Facets of Sight"
Pastel pencils on charcoal paper, 8x8 inches, 2013

This piece speaks to the innumerable facets of sight. Enriching layers of meaning through interpretation exist in the world, and I aspire to appreciate life as an encompassing sphere rather than a limiting circle.

Chestnut Review

VOLUME 4 NUMBER 2 AUTUMN 2022

Chestnut Review LLC, Ithaca, New York
chestnutreview.com

Chestnut Review appears four times a year online, in January, April, July, and October, and once per year in print in July.

ISSN 2688-0350 (online), ISSN 2688-0342 (print)

CONTENTS

Introduction

Fall is a wonderful time of year to take stock of where we are and celebrate past accomplishments while looking forward to the future. We published our anthology of Volume 3 recently and had an all-staff meeting that was full of information about the magazine and our direction. We also have celebrated the finalists and winners of the Stubborn Writers Contest, whom we look forward to publishing in the Winter Issue. Through various initiatives, we continue to build programs and think about how to reimagine our offerings for next year and beyond. We are pleased to announce that we will hold our first in-person retreat in Merida, Mexico, next January and that we will be developing more retreats that will allow our community to travel and write together. However, we have not forgotten the advantages that virtual collaboration and offerings afford, the equalization of opportunity that was one of the boons of the pandemic quarantine, so we are also continuing with chances to write and workshop in community with other CR writers, staff, and readers around the world. We thank you for reading us and writing with us, and we hope to continue serving stubborn artists for years to come. Here is our Fall Issue, with its autumnal twists, turns, and transformations. We hope you enjoy.

MARK BLACKFORD

A Conversation with Seif-Eldeine, Poetry Chapbook Winner

This year's chapbook contest was, for me, full of surprises and strength all throughout. Each year that I judge becomes more difficult, given the quantity and the quality of the work we receive, and I was certain that I had read the winner on numerous different occasions. That is, of course, until I came across Seif-Eldeine's *Voices From a Forgotten Letter: Poems on the Syrian Civil War.*

Seif-Eldeine's collection of poems is unique. It is special. Through numerous different voices and lenses, he does not simply give to us a portrait of a nation at war but, rather, the feeling of existing, when war seems to be all around you. Rather than going the typical "Western Media" route of keeping the focus on the atrocities and horrors of such a conflict, he brings us into the homes and lives of everyday Syrians, and he shows to us all that war is so much more than just soldiers fighting. These poems are delivered with such a cool head and even keel that one can't help but become immersed not just in the conflict, but in the ongoing everyday lives of people who, while not involved in the fighting, endure it as a part of their daily life, and accept that—war or not—their lives must still be lived.

I had the pleasure of speaking with Seif-Eldeine via Zoom, whilst locked away in a hotel room in Quantico, VA, and babysitting my infant son. These are two things I would recommend to NO ONE who may be trying to comfortably interview any individual, but we managed to pull it off. For your reading pleasure, I give you some of the highlights from our conversation below:

MB: So why don't we start with you telling us all a little bit about yourself, as the person and the writer?

S-E: Yeah! Well, I am a Syrian-American, and I am a huge Celtics fan. I have to mention that; that's a big part of my identity, too. Being Syrian is a big part of my identity. My dad grew up there and came here in 1981, and I was born in 1986. I visited there a lot when I was young. I went for the first time in 2001, and then multiple times after. The last I visited was 2009, and the war—the protests began in 2010—and the war began in 2011, so I was pretty close to that time.

MB: So you were there almost as the tension peaked, or when everything was coming to a loggerhead?

S-E: No. I was, like, right before that.

MB: Okay. And, as an aside, as a native New Yorker, I won't take issue with you being a Celtics fan. We all know that the Knicks suck. But does this also make you a Red Sox fan?

S-E: Yeah I am a Red Sox fan, so you got me beat with both of your teams. The Mets are good this year.

MB: They are! But all that means to any good Mets fan is that we're overdue for an implosion. We all know it's bound to happen. One of those "Don't trust to hope" kind of things.

But anyway, you were born in the States, but you had visited Syria numerous times through your young adulthood. This is very cool. Very interesting, because when I first read your collection, I had assumed that you were born and grew up in Syria. The reality of everything in the narrative had me dead certain that you were a native Syrian who had emigrated here, possibly at the start of—or during—the conflict.

S-E: Yeah . . . I took a lot of time, you know, taking in interviews; taking in documentaries; taking my own experiences and education. I was a Middle Eastern Studies major in college, so I was using that and a lot of elements that were just there, and happened to be useful at a time I think it's needed.

MB: I couldn't agree more. So where did you go to school?

S-E: I went to Tufts University.

MB: Very cool. So, was it like a part of your major to conduct a lot of these interviews, or was it a personal choice?

S-E: Neither, actually. I just looked into documentaries from outlets like Vice News, and interviews I found online. *The Washington Post* had a lot of great material. U.N. Aid actually had a lot of great material, like the detail about the pet pigeon in one of the poems, that is from an U.N. Aid advertisement.

MB: I did love the line with the pigeon. It gave such a more personal nature to that poem, and I think it really conveyed a sense of sparseness or scarcity to the front. So you kind of found all of these poems through various witness documentaries and interviews? Things any of us could have seen or found, but more than likely glossed over?

S-E: Yeah! And then I took the scaffolding of the poems from a lot of different—I would say—blue-collar American worker poets, like Phil Levine....

MB: There is definitely an air of Phil Levine and Larry Levis that I can grasp from reading your poems, and I think that kind of scaffolding helps to set the tone for this collection. I was very amazed at how even-keeled these poems are, especially given the weight and severity of the content. You keep such a level-headed tone that, no matter what was being shown or given to us, it seemed like just another day.
How did you manage that, especially with such heavy and emotionally personal content?

S-E: I think the better question might be: "How do I ever get out of that tone?" I try so hard to get out of that tone sometimes. It's just something that...it just comes natural to me. It's a tone that I work in. My second manuscript has a completely different tone from that. At that point, I wanted to grow into something different. I don't want to be repeating the same thing my whole career, and this is just the start.

MB: How much difficulty did you find transitioning all of this found material onto the page in the way you did? Was there much manipulation involved?

S-E: Not a lot. Not a lot. So, I sort of compartmentalize when I am writing. So I'll have the scaffolding from the imitation, then I'll have....Maybe I'll be looking at the article, and I'll take the information from the article and fit it into the syntax and the feeling, and the tone of the poem I am using as a model. And that makes it easier. But dude, I take YEARS to make edits on these poems. These poems are coming from, like, 11-12-13 years ago.

MB: I was certain of that. From what I know of the Syrian Civil War is that when the Obama Administration ended, it seemed like the major news sources all started to go: "Let's just close this thing out." It seemed to just fade out. And I am sure that it's a conflict that—if not still ongoing—has a long process of rebuilding ahead.

S-E: There is limited action currently. Right now, it's more of a refugee crisis, but there is still fighting in the north—in the Kurdish section—and in Halib, where a lot of terrorists are. But the government has retaken control of massive amounts of the country. So, the conflict is sort of limited nowadays.

So, I sort of process my emotions through my poetry a lot. In my day-to-day, I'm not thinking too much about the Syrian conflict or other things. I'm trying to relax because that work does take a mental toll if you're just doing it all day long. My job is like that. It's very emotionally challenging.

MB: What do you do, if you don't mind my asking?

S-E: I am a TMS Technician. I treat people with major depressive disorders. So I make sad people happy.

MB: Which can be a very emotionally draining thing.

Would you say, in your approach to your poetry, is it kind of a way of processing or offsetting that emotional drain?

S-E: Not really. It's more just processing my emotions and my thoughts and how I view the world. I was concerned about getting caught up in overarching narratives and such. I wanted to get down to different points. I tried to write from as many points of view as possible. I was trying to explore as many psyches as I possibly could.

MB: Which you certainly accomplish in this work. I am very excited to help get this book off the ground with you. You really do have a gift for voice, and for viewing.

So, the one question I ask to each writer is: What's the best piece of advice you can give to anybody who is working to publish a manuscript of poems, or just working to get themselves published? Really, to anyone who is trying to get themselves into this realm?

S-E: Honestly, if possible, get a job where you can write on the job. Or just write any way you can. Was it T.S. Eliot who used to write on the bank checks?

MB: I think that was William Carlos Williams. He used to write on the prescription pads.

S-E: Yeah. That's the best way. As a poet, you may not be looking for the most glamorous job, anyway, so something that will pay the bills and keep food on the table, and allow you extra time to write is just perfect.

Last Communion

Here I am, kneeling again before a man
who tells me I can be holy while insisting that nothing
is permanent, not even my precious sins.
I am washed in the blood, longing for something sacred,
tongue hanging over my bottom lip like a dog.

I like to read between the lines of obituaries, try
to guess what their family members left out on purpose.
You can tell a lot by what isn't there. For example,
vague obit of healthy teenager: death by overdose,
50-year-old mom who was a brave warrior: breast cancer,
30-year-old male, donations to NAMI in lieu of flowers: suicide.

My sister was an asshole, and now she's dead.
Though her life ended at 37, I wrote her eulogy
as though she died at age nine,
because that was the last time she wasn't an asshole,
and I wanted to say something true
without pissing everyone off.

Here's the thing—if all we have to do to erase
our gravest mistakes is take communion or stop breathing
one day, what is keeping us from making them all,
from relishing each one, knowing in the end,
they will not define us?

When I die, please tell everyone the truth about me.
That I walked around this place believing
I was a little better than most. That twice I turned away
from true love out of pride, revered books more
than men. That I did, in fact, have a favorite child.

While you're at it, reveal this truth about us all—
that each of us has secrets we take to the grave,
things we want to admit, but are certain no one wants to hear.
Tell them that the very last time I ever took communion,
I closed my lips around the priest's finger, let him
feel my hot tongue against his skin. And he let me.

Chichi and I

I am afraid for Chichi.

When cold darkness begins to creep around us in the evening, dotting goosebumps along our arms, she turns long and thin with fear; so long, so skinny that she is hard to perceive. When her fingers grow taller than my whole body, I know it is time to pull her by her hand to my room, where we curl under the little spring bed in the middle of my dark bedroom. I shrink her to peanut-sized and hold her in the shallow between my stomach and thighs until she falls asleep. She does not answer when I whisper her name. She does not show her face when I cry silently on the cold, dusty floor.

In the morning, my alarm shrills through my dreams, shredding each one into pieces so little that I can never reassemble them, no matter how hard I try. There were monsters, I remember, tall monsters with giant arms and big ears. They hid under my bed and came from around me, tearing through my struggling arms, trying to capture Chichi. She was not surprised and did not struggle; she never does, for she does not care whether she lives or dies, but I do.

The monsters tore her into pieces so little that she became nothing in my dreams, but she did not scream. She did not scream because she expected me to do it for her. I do everything for Chichi, and she does everything for me. This is why I am afraid for Chichi; because she does not know how to speak for herself, but I need her to speak for me.

I rise before she does with a shiver of panic. I peek out from under the sharp metal edge of my bed, slapping off the alarm and looking around to make sure nothing around me hurts her. I call her name silently, afraid that she is gone. But she is here with me; she always is. Chichi wakes up and, in the candlelight, rubs Vaseline all over her skin, exactly like I do, melting large dollops over her dry knees, down her shins to her ankles. She braids her hair, like I do, into two untidy cornrows that run from the top of the head, falling over the neck.

We do our best not to wake Papa up as we creep around our house. Chichi and I pull our uniforms from the hanging lines outside the kitchen door and put them on quietly, enjoying the freshly washed cotton on our skins. We tiptoe into the living room table, pick up pages of our neatly done school assignments, and stack them in our schoolbags.

On our way to school, with our uniforms squared up at the collar and our white stockings tight just below our knees, we walk by the village square, with doors chained across and the market stalls tightly roped shut. We walk around them, hoping to find fruits lying under the wooden poles that hold the market together.

Once we found eight bananas discarded under a stall, all wrinkled away from their bunch. They were blackened on the skin but sweet and juicy inside. It was a good day that one. We sat on a large rock and ate each one, pausing to take in the overly sweet smell after each bite. But today, we find nothing. We try to pry the ropes open to steal fruit, but Chichi is afraid that we will be caught and beaten to death like the pickpocket we saw one Wednesday, sitting on an old tire in the middle of a crowd. We wove our way between legs to get a view. His eyes were swollen shut, mouth dripping red, stones falling on his raw skin, one after the other. Chichi is afraid to die like the pickpocket, in the stinking blue flame of burning rubber, so we take one walk around the market, hoping to find discarded fruit instead. We find nothing, so I call Chichi along, and we continue the walk to school.

I remind Chichi to walk upright, to square her shoulders, and jut her chin because she sometimes slouches when I am not paying attention. We join up along a stream of similarly dressed kids, rushing to make time before the morning assembly bell. Some nod at us as a greeting and some hug us and choose to walk beside us. We do not care, Chichi and I, whether they leave us alone or run from us, for we are whole together. But we smile when they smile, we hug when they hug; we make conversation when they do.

Did you do your homework? asks a boy with grey uniform shorts that hug his thick thighs and ride in towards a gather around his crotch.

We nod yes, Chichi and I, for we always do our homework. It doesn't matter how we do it, but we always do our homework. Sometimes under the shadowy glow of a lantern, sometimes under the moonlight.

He raises his hands, both thumbs up. Good for you, he says, Mr. Serem does not take any excuses for incomplete homework.

We join the procession from the barred school gate to the school assembly, with our shoes polished exactly as they should be. Chichi is afraid because we used saliva to polish our shoes, spitting on them and rubbing till they shone. But I tell her not to worry. Nobody knows, Chichi, I whisper; nobody knows that our kiwi shoe polish dried out in its can, so we could not use it. Nobody knows that we wiped our faces clean with dew from the grass outside our house. Nobody cares enough to know, Chichi. Trust me.

The teacher asks us to open our books, and we shut our

mouths through maths, about long divisions and isosceles triangles. Chichi wants to speak, but I hold her lips shut through the maths class, English class, and Christian Religious Education class, where the teacher in a flowered purple skirt that grazes her ankles talks about how God loves us so much that He gave His only son. I only hold Chichi's lips tight because I am afraid for her. I need for her to be unnoticeable. But she wants to swell, Chichi. She wants to raise her hand to ask, Does he really love us, this God you speak about? How could he love us and make us suffer at the same time? But I slap her hands down and lock them between my thighs. Remember, Chichi, I say, our only defence is to be invisible.

Over midday break, when the sun is up and my friends shout my name through the window to come out to play, Chichi rushes out from under me and runs ahead. At that moment, she seems strong and invincible. She bounces off walls and slides down staircases. She swings in the playground, over and under the rusty iron bars. My friends chant songs of admiration at us, daring us to swing higher, to ride faster, to screech louder, and Chichi does, grabbing the bars by her toes and jumping from one to the next like a little monkey. My friends clap their hands and round their mouths to perfect Os and widen their eyes. I jump along with Chichi, the warmth of the sun kissing my thighs when my dress flies over my shoulders and covers my face. I scream and laugh too, but only I can see through the façade: Chichi is breakable, like a wooden toy.

Over lunch, we watch with watering mouths as other pupils open their lunch boxes. Chichi and I stand in the corner as aromas of spicy pilau, oily mandazi, and steamed sweet potatoes attack our nostrils. We linger, dancing around the metal poles that hold the lunch hall together. We hear shouts—Please join us, my mother packed more than I can eat!—but I grab Chichi by her waist and tell her that our pride is more important than our hunger, even though we haven't had a proper meal for days.

After school, we walk back home through the woods, and Chichi wants to stop to climb a tree with a wide trunk and branches sneering at the sky. I let her because Chichi loves to be her own person, to swing like a monkey. She hangs over branches, dancing from one tree to the next, picking up wild fruits and shoving them in her mouth. I let her because I am hungry too. The loquats are sweet and sour, the guavas are soft to dig into, and the mangoes are so sweet that one bite stings our ears. The juices run down our chins, staining our collars.

When we get home, Papa sits on the porch, screaming at imaginary people, throwing beer cans at us, swearing about our dirty uniforms, cursing about why he is tied to us and never free. I am afraid because I can protect Chichi from everything, but not this.

<u>NJOKU NONSO</u>

Pray the Elegy

Atop a frozen lake, we dug through seasons past
and gone, leftovers of a bombed world. The bones
of our hands, steel-cold and full of weight like
a tongue in distress. Bloodworms in a litany of ice.
We dug for little, little things, that would make
each of our nine lives bearable. We christened
the performance: Burying the Chaos. Watched
our garden of teeth grow rotten-dark with longing.
What keeps alive Arabian pilgrims who carry jars
of water that would not last them three hundred
and sixty walks across the desert. All day, we dug
for the harvest of a joy-wet world. What was our
kingdom before the war became a spell of flood.
Yet no one, not even the Almighty Seer, told us
whatever we had wanted was no longer there—
at the wild gate-end of our suffering: a ghost-face
trapped inside a ghost-town—a road trailblazing
through a forest of things. Neat gold coins jangling
inside our trouser pockets. Mid-afternoon housetop
views of a new world nesting outside the wicked
mouth of a homeless bullet. A sonnet that turns
a broken tooth into a hail of silver into a soft shimmer
in the midnight lake. O borderless mirror O eyelids
snapped shut against this blade of tattered glass,
of what use is living if we are all moving graveyards?

ISIBEAL OWENS

Busted Cantaloupe: Pilgrim

The orange meat is splayed open
in the parking lot of Whole Foods—
angry and naked like the corpse
of a virgin. Minivan moms go stomping
through with their galoshes. They leave
sticky prints in the grass. Ants frack
the soil for their queen's supper—gold
has been struck. The queen is now whisky
drunk off glucose. The venom
in her pinchers runs sweet.
Her drool sinks into the earth,
into magma. Sunset blends
with sunset, and loam descends to mantle.
An underwater volcano spits it out off the coast
of Australia. The corals are going chalky grey.
Along the reef, a surviving clownfish feels faint.
Haunted by asphalt. The drone
of car engines and crack pipes.
Another life flashes before its eyes:
seeds and fingers and hot red moons.
The knives slice fire into metal and obsidian
into rust. Bricks bundled like runt babies. Our
world, a cavity along a candy necklace. Bleed
juice into blender, potion into gut.

Held between incisor and oblivion.
Click jaws into flesh.
Melt.

TAYLOR YINGSHI

"Subway Characters #3"
Digital drawing, 6x9 inches, 2022
(Next Page)

I stayed at a friend's place in Brooklyn all summer. It was a one
hour subway ride between the apartment and the place I was
working, so I had plenty of time to sketch. I thought, live draw-
ing classes are like $100, why not DIY it with the added challenge
that your subject could move positions at any point!? I ended up
learning a lot not only about the technical side of figure drawing,
but also the minute details—a scuffed watch, an asymmetrical
earring—that add to a person's aesthetic and often reveal a lot
about them.

ABDULJALAL MUSA ALIYU

Delineation of a Woman's First Child as Her True Religion

When Boko Haram beat the drums of
Jihad, my brother—with a university degree,

high-paying job & family that worshipped
him—joined the dance. That was when

it dawned on me that, belief, like wildfire,
destroys every single leaf of reasoning

that sets foot on its field. Sadness fli-
tted on our mother's skin like a moth.

& that made me remember when I
protested that the difference between

the love she had for my brother & me, was
like the distance between heaven &

earth, & she said—with a smile wide
enough to drown the history of mankind

in its fount—that a woman's first child
is her true religion. Now we fill our

mouths with a handful of silence when
we dine, for every word we speak

reminds us of him: of how his jokes cut
through everyone else's like a sword; of

how he would taste everyone's food—
except father's—like the content

were dissimilar; of how, after he grad-
uated, before every meal, we had to

whisper into God's ears his need to be
richer than Dangote. Our father once

asked that we prayed to God to bend
his heart towards the truth, towards

his love that was threatening to trans-
form our household into a graveyard of

silence. Before a word could fall from
anyone's mouth, mother's tears had

dropped on the dining table. That was
the first time I saw proof of heartbreak;

like a full moon in a blue sky. It is dis-
heartening—like death—how one person's

decision could set a whole family on fire.
You see, I deleted all the social media

platforms on my phone, for how could I
hold onto the devils that made a monster

out of my brother? Two years later, he
dropped into our home, tattered, as though

flung by hurricane. Mother fell into the
arms of her long lost son in tears of joy.

& father stood like a statue; paralyzed by
surprise laced with ecstasy. He did not

make use of more than twenty words—in
twenty-four hours—in his new dialect of

half sign language & half muteness. I
saw happiness fading away from my

parents' faces like a hatchling's skin. &
when we sat down to eat, he said no

word should crawl towards why he left—
he had sunk all his jovial essence in a pit

that screamed of sadness. I do not know
how to say—without my words carrying

shadows of resentment—that, I crave
the company of my brother whose spirit

was murdered by this stranger. When we
woke—the following day—he left us a

letter that read: you infidels should walk
back to God. My mother locked herself in

her room, sopping in the waters of grief &
tears. & when my father hugged me, our

tears drenching each other's shoulders,
I whispered in his ear: your other son is

dead, & we need to find a way to bury him
in a cemetery far away from our hearts.

MATINA VOSSOU

"Your Pain Is My Pain But Your Pleasure Isn't Mine"
Acrylics on paper postcard using toothpicks, 7.48x5.11 inches, 2022
(Next Page)

The piece that I am submitting is part of my new and ongoing collection "Postcards From A Postponed Posterity". They are all painted portraits on plain postcards (19 cm X 13 cm) using toothpicks and acrylics. Smaller size but same aesthetic and vision. Like any other typical postcard, these ones also carry a written message for a title; a verse, an introductory sentence or maybe a parable, for the better understanding of the facial expression and the situation that this person is in. The specific portrait was inspired from a black and white photograph which caught my eye immediately for its dark quality. It brought to my mind the idea of somebody very nervous, trying to hide his face from the world. It seems like he is watching from a distance jealously somebody special to him. But something really deep, a rejection or a denial, is eating him up inside.

LANA HALL

Paying for It

The night bylaw officers raid our massage parlour, we flee out the back like ants, snow crunching underfoot, sequins flashing under our winter coats. It's a slow night and there's nothing criminal about sitting in the dressing room of a massage parlour, but I follow the lead of my coworkers, fleeing not just the law, but the strangely intimate rituals of being policed. Once, I saw Hannah in the hallway during a raid, shivering in a bedsheet as an officer wrote her a ticket for being underdressed. *You couldn't pay me to do your job*, he said, the sound of the ticket being ripped from the pad, like a whip.

Wading through the parking lot, Martina grabs my parka and yanks me down behind a truck with her. For the briefest of seconds, a bolt of glee flashes through my body, before it collides with something that makes my stomach clench. We're out here because we've taken a wrong turn, wanted the worst things. Back inside, a wall of men is waiting to remind us of this. We watch some coworkers hop the fence and scatter across the street, probably heading to the 24-7 coffee shop where they'll have to dodge truckers' advances for the next hour. Aisha's still in a room doing who knows what with her client. *Godspeed to her.* The auto body shop beside the parlour is closed, so we settle in behind a bank of rusted-out cars and check our phones, waiting for the all-clear. I feel Martina's breath on my neck, smell the burnt caramel of her body lotion as we watch the crack of light coming from the parlour's back door, the cold rippling across our exposed skin. *What a load of shit*, she says. *If I had a cop on my massage table, he'd enjoy it just as much as any other man.*

In high school, I had a job cleaning rooms at a two-star motel where Gina, our head housekeeper, warned me the maintenance guy would snatch housekeepers' tips from the nightstands before they could pocket them. Sun leaked through tattered curtains as we cleaned: pools of coffee grunge, discarded syringes, a nacho explosion trapped in shag carpet, and Gina's bony dishrag hands scrubbing away, the flash of faded tattoos on her forearms. *I use those goddamn tips to buy snacks for my kids*, she muttered. But we needed that job and the maintenance guy knew it, so we let it slide. We all figure out how to survive, one way or another.

Before I learned how to take the money and run, I learned how to give it up.

The entire strip mall's gone dark for the night, and soon, we will too. We're doing math in our heads, hoping we made enough money earlier on shift, because even after the officers leave, slushy footprints and the red glow of electric bulbs in their wake, the parlour will be a dead zone. Word gets out fast, and nobody's looking for a good time if they know law enforcement's out.

Behind us the main drag stretches out, where during the day fuel tankers rattle along, drivers in pickups cut between highways, swerve into drive-thrus for food they devour hunched at the wheel, salt and grease staining their palms. It's a road people only take on their way somewhere else. Awash in darkness it defies time and place, a reminder that we don't always know which detours we'll take as we move through the world. I pull my gaze from it and catch Martina's eye. Suddenly, we're laughing. We try not to blow our cover, grabbing each other's arms in hysteria, muffling the sounds on our jacket sleeves, but this only makes us laugh harder. It feels so ridiculous, the idea that every life choice we've ever made has led us to this moment: huddling in the dark, half-naked behind a thicket of junk cars, hiding from a bunch of officers who are probably just trying to pay their own bills and head home to the early morning oatmeal and quiet lawns of their suburban homes. Giddiness blooms in the cold winter air, tangible as the clouds of our breath. Wiping her eyes, Martina lights a cigarette and takes a drag, burgundy lipstick staining the end. The moon is high. Nobody can touch us.

<u>MAYA HERSH</u>

do you see me

the heat rolls in waves across seattle,
breaks us into pieces,

the south end loses power again while the mayor
eats sushi and smiles for the camera,
my boss
owns two cars and bikes to work,
sits in the air-conditioned office while the factory floor
melts into lava and engulfs us,
we turn our faces to the fans and work until we drop
and they replace us,
need another body in the raw room, guys,
this one is toast.

there are cooling centers in the morgue down the street from me.
we joke
on break, it's so hot in here it would be worth it, just
slide me into that fridge baby,
let me lie down a while.
we hold our meetings in the office (usually
off limits)
because my manager can't think in the heat i am working in,
he says, go home if you feel sick
as long as you're hitting targets.

once, we hired and fired so many people in the same week that i
forgot
to learn their names.
i think one
was elijah,
he was so excited about free food in the break room
he poured all the coffee creamer on his cereal, ate it standing and
gesticulating,
he didn't last long.
my manager chides us about the rates of a person
they fired last year, our faces
must seem such a blur to them, the office people,
the ones who aren't sweating,
they shuffle us like pawns with a click of their spreadsheets
just another expense to try to minimize,

my neighbor
layers tinfoil over all her windows to keep the sun out,
no one is selling air conditioners right now, except
the expensive ones,
like the one my boss bought
for his home
when the heat wave hit,
the factory floor reaches 94 degrees,
i go home sick and feel guilty for days,
drink water like it is a chore,
got to get back before they forget about me,
got to keep my body away from that cooling center,
keep my name on that paycheck,
it's only getting hotter.

Decay

Don't marry a banana slug, my mother said. No good can come of it, she said. But I was young and in love with the way his flaxen body glistened in the sun.

I met him while hiking in the woods just north of the city. I had just lost another temp job I thought might go permanent, and my mom had called to tell me my dad's cancer had returned but not to worry, he was responding to the chemo.

I needed to clear my head.

The trail was slick with rain, the ground squelching here and there underfoot. Eyes and thoughts unfocused, accompanied only by the sound of my well-worn boots on wet debris, I rounded a bend and nearly stepped on him. I would have if he hadn't yelled, *Hey!*

I looked down and there he was, his optical tentacles quivering in my direction. I apologized for nearly flattening him, and he told me no harm done. He introduced himself as *A. dolichophallus* but said I could call him A. I introduced myself as Beatrice and said he could call me B. His body rippled, but I couldn't tell if he'd gotten the joke. He asked what I was doing in his neck of the woods and said the rhythm of my footsteps, which he'd felt through the ground, seemed somber. He was sensitive to those kinds of things. I found myself spilling my heart onto the forest floor. He seemed a most attentive listener, though he had no face for me to read. He asked follow-up questions, and we talked for a long time.

When the light through the canopy of trees grew dim, I told him I had to go, and he said he hoped our paths might cross again. I continued my damp trek toward civilization feeling lighter.

I came back the next day to find A perched on a rotting log a few feet from where I'd left him, a sticky, luminescent trail in his wake. He was happy to see me, he said. I went back every day after that.

On drier days, I would often find A submerged in a mound of dead leaves, spots of yellow peeking through the brown foliage. Sometimes he asked me to bring him treats, and I would grab whatever aspirational produce was decomposing in my crisper— moldy strawberries, slimy mushrooms, wilted lettuce. He could turn decay into rich soil just by eating it, he said. A little, breathing compost bin. He nibbled slowly on my offerings with his microscopic teeth while I lay on my back on the moldering ground watching the light filter through the trees, content to just be with him. When he finished whatever I had brought him, he would always ask for more. I felt the rasp of his long, tooth-covered tongue exploring my elbow, my neck, the back of my knee. Looking for a taste of me.

We couldn't have sex in a human way. Banana slugs are a hermaphroditic species and can self-fertilize when they need to, so he was pretty self-sufficient in that respect, A said. I said I was pretty self-sufficient too, that I'd been masturbating a long time, but that I wanted to be close to him. He suggested that we rub up against each other, so I lay down on the dank earth and tried to make my right hand as slug-like as possible. He rubbed his sensory tentacles and then his body against my cupped palm, back and forth in an undulating, muculent dance that lasted hours. I grew heady from his moans, dizzy from his scent. Pheromones, he moaned, as I slid my left hand beneath the waistband of my leggings. When it was over, I gently peeled his small body from my own, the slime almost an adhesive between us. He asked if he could eat my penis, and I explained that I didn't have one. How curious, he said.

A liked the feel of my tongue, and I spent long afternoons licking the mucus along his back, tonguing his shuddering pneumostome until my mouth numbed and he absorbed all its moisture. He needed my moisture to make more mucus, he said, the one time I complained through desiccated lips. The taste was bitter, but I liked making him happy, loved feeling valuable. Afterward, I'd replenish with a yellow Gatorade, imagining I was drinking his essence.

After several weeks, he proposed. When I told my mom the news, she cried and hung up on me.

A and I married in a quiet ceremony in the woods as near as we could remember to the spot where I'd almost trampled him. I found a guy on Craigslist who'd been ordained online and was willing to perform the ceremony in exchange for leaving him in the woods with two cases of light beer, which seemed like a bargain.

After the ceremony, I placed A in the back of my old station wagon, in the terrarium I had made, and drove to my apartment. We decided to split our time between the city and the forest. He curiously absorbed all the new sights and sounds, but when we got to my studio he seemed vaguely disappointed, slowly turning his ocular tentacles around to take in the small space.

Is this all there is? he asked.

Yes, I said. This is all there is.

Things changed. He grew distant, stopped listening, and constantly criticized my terrarium-keeping skills. But I longed to please him, to feel again that sticky pull between us. I still licked him, sometimes multiple times a day, though now he preferred for me to do it from behind him while he watched videos of banana slugs on my propped-up cell phone. I licked until my breath grew sour. Until my teeth began to rot.

We are back in the forest now, and my body has grown parched, skin shriveled all over like the pad of a finger left too long in the bath.

Perhaps, like my mother, you are thinking I should have seen it sooner, that it is A's nature to long for my decay. And perhaps you are right.

When I speak, which isn't often now, my voice crackles like dead leaves, and my tongue is a chip of bark inside my mouth. If you asked me a question, you'd have to lean in close to hear the answer, close enough to smell moldering flesh, the hint of sweetness underneath. You'd have to put your ear right up to my dry, cracked lips. You'd have to listen very carefully. Maybe then you would hear me tell you that I wouldn't change a thing.

CLAIRE SCOTT

THE SEA SQUIRT LOSES ITS MIND

It eats its own brain
once attached headfirst to a rock
where it will spend the rest of its brief life
the brain no longer needed since
it's never going to move again

I recently settled in Sunset Lodge
last stop assisted living
in Walnut Creek, California
living a sessile existence
in a minuscule apartment

On the windowless sixteenth floor
never going anywhere again
no trips to science museums
wobbling on a walker
no beach vacations
dipping bunioned toes in salty brine

I sit in my chair all day
roots burrowing into blind earth
staring at wallpaper roses

while neurons blink out like morning stars
someone who looks like my daughter
says try yoga or tai chi

But my body barely moves anymore
my mind no longer scribbles memories
living between world and not world
yet I am alive, still alive inside my skin
counting rows and rows of pink roses

An LSAT of Culture

Please read the passage and brief statement below. The question that follows is based on the reasoning contained in the passage and statement. The correct answer is the response that most accurately and completely answers the question. You should not make assumptions that are by commonsense standards implausible, superfluous, or incompatible with the passage and/or statement.

Mr. Lin is one of Mr. Wang's most efficient and valuable partners. In each of the past three years, Mr. Lin, on his own, has generated at least $2.5 million in revenue for the company, and this is excluding the indirect impacts he's had on the franchise, such as scouting the right talents at the right time, brand-building, and fostering a healthy relationship among co-workers that does not involve the words *cao ni ma* and *qu ni da ye de*. Due to his outstanding, if not extraordinary performance, Mr. Wang offered to buy him a luxury sports car.

"No, Old Wang, I can't take it," Mr. Lin said, pushing away the sports car pamphlet in Mr. Wang's hands.

"Oh, come on Old Lin, this is the bare minimum I can do to show my appreciation," Mr. Wang said, pushing the pamphlet back to Mr. Lin. "Pick one."

"You know I'm not all about the money, Old Wang. Seeing our company get better each and every day is what motivates me," Mr. Lin said. He took the pamphlet and slid it into Mr. Wang's pants pocket.

"Okay, fine, I know you're a clean fella. How about this: It's almost Christmas, and I will add $50,000 to your end-of-year bonus. You have to give me some face, Old Lin." Mr. Wang placed a hand in his own pocket and shoved the pamphlet deeper in.

Mr. Lin stared at the half-lit cigarette between his fingers, looking troubled. Then he looked up at Mr. Wang, let out a deep sigh, and said, "All right, if you so insist. Why you always gotta be so courteous, Old Wang?"

The two men laughed, patted each other on the shoulder, and went on to talk about other things.

On the night of the end-of-the-year banquet, after everyone had already left, a buzzed Mr. Wang came up to Mr. Lin.

"Old Lin, I was thinking," Mr. Wang called, his tone as cordial as ever, "our company will be in a bit of a tight spot next year. We have the Infinity One project and the Flying Tiger project lined up. We really need to save up. You'll surely understand if I temporarily withhold $10,000 from your bonus, right? The remainder is still plenty."

Mr. Lin patted Mr. Wang on the back and smiled, "Of course, Old Wang. I already told you I'm not all about the money."

"That's good," Mr. Wang said, "That's good." The two men walked together to the station, all the while laughing and joking about the evening's events.

When Mr. Lin returned home, he ignored his wife, disregarded his children's greetings, and headed directly to his bedroom. Once the door was shut behind him, he threw a wine glass across the room, shattering it into pieces. He shouted, "Cao ni ma, qu ni da ye de, you short, little fat fuck."

The above was the draft of a story I submitted to a flash fiction workshop. After my fellow American writers had finished reading it, they nodded, grinned, and moaned in a way that poets do after hearing a delicious sequence of words. Yet, during the critique session, mostly everybody was silent; they kept on flipping back and forth between the pages, scratching their heads, as if searching for something in my story. Of the two writers that did comment, one suggested I flesh out the characters a bit more. "Wang and Lin are such interesting people. I so want to learn more about them." The other asked what kind of sports cars were in the pamphlet that Mr. Wang originally handed to Mr. Lin. "My wife drives a Maserati, and I tell ya, it's a heck of a lot more expensive than $50,000."

Which of the following statements, if true, would most help to explain the apparent discrepancy in **both** the aspiring writer's story and his experience in the flash fiction workshop?

(A) Despite what Mr. Lin says, he is actually all about the money.

(B) Despite Mr. Wang's courtesies, he doesn't actually want to give Mr. Lin any money—not even a penny.

(C) Despite what it seems to suggest, the whole point of the $50,000 is to show that Mr. Wang actually lowered his initial offer of the sports car (in a rather unobtrusive and shady manner, of course).

(D) Despite what the aspiring writer may believe, he is not actually a good writer, and his story is not of publishable quality.

(E) It's often said that the Great Dragon of the East has a beautiful and rich history of 5,000 years, and in the realms of this intricate culture, one frequently has to say the opposite of what he wants and leave his true intentions to the common sense of the interpreter. It's often said that the Land of the Free and Home of the Brave is one that values freedom of speech and press. This is a nation founded on justice and liberty, and after nearly two hundred and fifty years of development, the land has become a melting pot of cultures and traditions with opportunities for various people to thrive. Yet despite what is often said and their sincere efforts, the writers in the aspiring writer's workshop ultimately failed to give a shit about his story.

DENNY MARSHALL

"Curl of the Sting"
B&W ink, 6x9 inches, 2021

Many artists out there create works that look all the same. While some of my works look similar, in the end my number one goal is for my artwork not to look all the same when taken as a whole. After that I like to get emotion, movement, or depth if not all three at least one of them.

GUY D'ANNOLFO

The long call of yearning

Everything that comes from wishing is foreign to us.
-Seneca

Drizzle obscures sunset as if it had never
fully risen, a legato call stills
the charcoal hillside, a dripping staccato response;
owls make argument enchanting in the botanical

garden, carved out of the town by a surveyor,
while an excision chart is drawn around
my palate's cancer site; your reason to live:
to raise my son with love and compassion.

After a boundless night, I woke the sun,
it glided past my petition with burning indifference,
without a word I struggle to catch breath;

I'll stand with it, to true my shadow at noon,
to accept that life knows usefulness and beauty
only by cutting the long call of yearning short.

BISWADARSHAN MOHANTY

Djinn and Men

By a fire in a Bedouin camp
not far from date fronds
kahwa[1] dripped through the sky's fine mesh
trickled through the Milky way
into cups, emanating fumes of cardamom,
coffee and stories
that cracked with embers on which djinn danced.
Djinn, the beings of fire, tolerated
men and their stories,
for the two beings shared same longings,
same vices, same wickedness.

Behind the row of men and tents
were lines of dunes that
shifted in day and ruminated at night.
They were simpler creatures
made neither of mud nor fire,
but of sand.
Sand that rises in dervishes,
dribbles into an hourglass
filling emptiness—
sprouting tents of glass and steel
stacked one on top of the other.
From their perches in one such tent,

men and women inhale foamy decoctions and
through a screen of clear sand
watch sand drape over
what remains of their horizon.

Djinn still lurk in the desert,
and in leather-bound
Alif Layla wa-Layla and
turn blue in Hollywood musicals—
they also skulk in the city,
in windowless massage parlours
under red-blue neon signs
flashing OPEN
in not so dark alleyways,
where men ask,
"How Much?"

---

[1] Kahwa—Arabic Coffee

E I L E E N   F R A N K E L   T O M A R C H I O

Sudden Evolution

Oh, hello, whale! my daughter calls out to the sky. I look up at a thunderhead just blocking the sun. Low riding with bucket dumps, a blot on a beach day. I hurry her into the boardwalk arcade with its musty sea critter carpeting and tumbling bells like pocket change. We buy Italian ices and play *Jurassic Park* pinball and wait for the thunder cracks.

Alice knocks the pinball machine with her tiny hipbones, buoyant, eager for the storm. I only feel the heaviness of low pressure. I wonder why she talked to the sky like she did, since she's never been one to see shapes in clouds. Since she's more earthbound, a digger. Always excavating for the worst, brushing the dirt from the quieted voices she hears, the scrolled headlines lifted intact. The TV, my phone, my ex.

Rare right whale spotted in Shrewsbury River, tangled in ghost nets. Humpback near Barnegat Light struck dead by freighter. Breeding cows starve due to diminished herring stocks from warming Atlantic.

It's hard to talk around the worst while she's in earshot, to use sighs, tsks, hmms. When she probes, I can only shrug or deflect because I don't have answers and can't pretend that I do. To cure her of her scowling jags, I help her find books about whales at the library. She loves measuring our land-creature smallnesses against their immensities, reciting breathless factoids as if awe on its own is enough to solve all problems. Whale song that can drift 10,000 miles, sperms boasting the largest brains ever on earth, blues big enough to swallow two brachiosauruses, three wooly mammoths, four tyrannosauruses. Big enough to be clouds.

My own awe comes out forced next to hers, my sincerity a shell. She wants more from me, I know, so that I'll be right alongside her. But I can't get there, as much as I try. I throw compliments heavenward as a way to mask my copping out. *She's made of better stuff than I am. Her generation will save us all. If I were her age, my marine-life icon would probably be SpongeBob.* I make Alice into something other. A creature not from me. Because how else could such a fluke, such a wonder, share my DNA?

From inside the arcade, we hear odd sounds. The gasps and cries of boardwalkers, yet no pelt of raindrops, no thunder. Alice takes my hand and leads me out into the dimmed daylight, our steps floaty. It's clear the storm is no storm at all but an exchange of water for air, molecule by molecule, droplet by droplet. We look up to see a cetacean sky. Humpbacks and rights and sperms and blues. Belugas and narwhals in rows like scales in mackerel clouds. And above the whales, the old sky, now the stratosphere. Spouts from blowholes that dart like comet tails. True clouds slight as brushstrokes. A shrunken, liquid sun. All so distant from here at the bottom of a sea that is slowly giving birth to itself.

Out of reflex, I lick my Italian ice; it dissolves to salt on my tongue. Alice levitates from the boards, laughing, waving her hands fin-like up at the whales. She's not scared, not at all. Her awe is immense. So immense it seems to suck what oxygen is left around me. My lungs strain. I ask her what'll happen to us, tiny bubbles trapping my voice. She gives a hurried answer in words interspersed with whistles and clicks. Something about how since whales were once land walkers, the same logic could mean we humans will have new, larger lungs to stay underwater without drowning. I want to tell her this is impossible. That evolution doesn't work that way, so fast.

But I can't say this because the world has turned more water than air, and bubbles can't hold my words anymore or contain my ignorance. *So this must be what dying out is*, I think, remembering a video I saw once. The history of Earth in three minutes, charted eastward from Los Angeles to New York City. Humanity emerging at the tail end, in New Jersey, from under the Hudson, peaking in Midtown Manhattan. And then the afterward, the assumed next notch on the timeline. Our drowning in the East River at three minutes and some odd seconds as a new epoch rises.

I look around at all the shore people so confused and puffed and large-eyed, lost in schools of herring and squid, in drifting gyres of arcade prizes and Whac-A-Mole mallets. From far away, a mournful sound reaches my rupturing eardrums. It's Alice, singing right next to me. She gazes with one marble eye, her fusing feet swishing like a tail, building force. I know she's pleading with me to evolve with her, but all I can do is shrug and make shreds of the Italian ice paper cup, release them like ghost guppies. I feel whittled as driftwood, the dead end of a branch.

Before I can touch the baby barnacles on her skin, Alice launches herself up, up toward the surface. I make a hollow effort to follow in her slipstream, to catch up, but only get so far with my feeble kicks, with the crush of fathoms above me. Her song trails behind her, faint. I blink and blink to see her better, tears becoming ocean. My daughter, about to breach for air. And a whale cow brushing close, taking her for her own, as if it's the natural order of things. As if she were always hers, never mine.

MOTOSCOPE
CYCLEMASTER COFFEE CO.

Cyclemaster Coffee Co.

Digitally manipulated original photo using MS Photos, Google Photos, and Comica software/photo filters, 3000x2250 mp, 2022
Portland, Oregon, USA

This work is a digitally manipulated photo that was created to honor the location of The Artist's inaugural "bucket list" solo show June-July, 2022, located on an inner-city highway in North Portland. A 16"x 20" canvas print of this work remains, gracing a prominent interior wall.

Semper Augustus

I can believe that tulips were once
worth much more than gold
that the beauty of a broken bloom moved
the sinews of men dressed exclusively in black
with silver buckles. Semper Augustus wore red
and white stripes—left them open-mouthed, a
pepperminted sweet, white cracked, like an egg,
showing the blood of birth inside, the drama of
carnal coloring, a simple vein calling to mind
the spark of embryonic sash, the yoke lain
on the shoulders of gamblers and wishers.
The word tulip means turban and the leaves
like sheathes of prayerful hands. Is to pray
to supplicate? Or to sacrifice oneself
to the antediluvian pull of petaled poetry
written with a pen only a creator could
fathom? I like the idea of a status symbol rolled
in dirt and quick to perish. How humble it seems,
compared to self-driving cars or meta-universes.
The romance of a flower with hardly a scent.
A tulip keeps growing after it's cut, keeps opening
and closing as night stalks day it sleeps and wakes
with its watcher, getting longer and longer,
"leggy" we say as it creeps farther from the

vase, searching out the golden coins of sun.
Heads rolled when the market crashed against
the northern shores. Bulbs betrothed to futures
were exposed to be marauding garlic or shallots,
their oniony breaths caught stinking of hope
for ease. We shun those who search for ease, but
really why should we? Isn't it hard enough
to push through the soil, to come back every year?

CONTRIBUTORS

Abduljalal Musa Aliyu is a school teacher and poet. Perhaps, if he were born as a lower animal, he would come as a bird - considering how much he loves being free. He writes from Zaria, Nigeria. His work appears or is forthcoming in *PIN, Ninshar Arts, 3 of Cups Press 2021 Anthology* and elsewhere. His piece won third prize in PIN's 2020 Poetically Written Prose Contest. He rants on Twitter @ AbduljalaalMusa.

Noel Cheruto is a Kenyan writer whose work has appeared in Harvard's *Transition Magazine, PRISM International, The Boston Review, Short Fiction Journal, Strange Horizons, Isele Magazine, Hotel Africa Anthology, Yellow Means Stay Anthology, Johannesburg Review of Books, Kikwetu Journal, On the Premises Magazine,* and elsewhere. She won Silver in the Short Story Day Africa Contest. She was named a finalist in the Aura Estrada Short Story Competition and was longlisted for the Afritondo Short Fiction Contest and the Commonwealth Short Story Prize. Noel lives in Nairobi.

Guy D'Annolfo (M.A.), after writing four novels and countless poems, started reading evolutionary biology to keep up with his son's interest in natural history; mixing in loads of Eastern poetry & thought he found a distinct voice and is now looking to share his poetry with a wider audience. Guy's had poems published by the *Cape Cod Times,* and now *Chestnut Review,* and expects to keep submitting until the list grows long.

Joan Kwon Glass is the mixed-race, Korean American author of NIGHT SWIM (Diode Editions, 2022) & three chapbooks. She serves as Editor-in-Chief for *Harbor Review,* as a Brooklyn Poets Mentor, is a proud Smith College graduate & has been a public school educator for 20 years. She serves on the faculty of Hudson Valley Writers Center & the Fine Arts Work Center of Provincetown. Her work has won or been a finalist for several prizes & her poems have been nominated for the Pushcart Prize & Sundress Anthology *Best of the Net.* Joan's poems have been published or are forthcoming in *Prairie*

Schooner, Asian American Writer's Workshop (The Margins), RHINO, Rattle, Dialogist & elsewhere. Please follow her on Twitter @joanpglass and see her website at www.joankwonglass.com. She lives in Connecticut with her family.

Lindsey Morrison Grant, self-identifying as a neurodivergent, two-spirit, elder storyteller and contrarian deeply rooted in the roar and lore that's become Portlandia of The Left Coast, attribute success and survival (if not salvation) to superlative supports, mindfulness practice and daily creative expression in words, sounds and images. Their word is currently represented by The SIY GALLERY of San Francisco. https://siygallery.com/collections/lindsey-morrison-grant.

Lana Hall is a writer based in Toronto, Canada whose work often examines the intersection of equity, labour, and the politics of urban life. Her journalism and essays have been published in *The Globe and Mail, Maisonneuve, Catapult, Spacing Magazine, Parhelion Literary Magazine*, and elsewhere. She is writing a memoir about her time working in the massage parlour business.

Maya Hersh is east coast born but made for Seattle, where she now resides and intends to spend the rest of her days. She has competed nationally as a slam poet since 2015, and has both coached and competed in the National Poetry Slam, Individual World Poetry Slam and Women of the World Poetry Slam, as well as competing and featuring at local shows across the United States. She has been published in *Pangaia Magazine, Space City Underground*, and *They Call Us*.

Rachel Lastra is a writer and editor currently based in the Pacific Northwest. Her work has also appeared in *SmokeLong Quarterly* and *MoonPark Review*. She is a student in the MA in Writing program at Johns Hopkins University.

Mike Yunxuan Li's writings have appeared or are forthcoming in *The Normal School, Tahoma Literary Review, Fourth Genre, Berkeley Fiction Review*, and other publications. He likes music from the classic rock era and is an enthusiast of vinyl records.

Jessie Zechnowitz Lim is a florist by day and poet by night, living in California on unceded Ohlone land. She holds an MA in Art History. Her work has been published or is forthcoming in *California Quarterly*, *The Indianapolis Review*, *The Ekphrastic Review*, *FEED*, *Litbreak Magazine*, *The Bold Italic*, and *Mother Mag*.

Denny E. Marshall has had art, poetry, and fiction published. Some recent credits include cover art for *Typehouse Magazine* Jan. 2022, and poetry in *Page & Spine* April 2022. See more at www.dennymarshall.com.

Biswadarshan Mohanty, having moved around numerous cities and countries, has found a home in his imagination. He is a graduate of Master of Arts in Writing and Literature from Deakin University. His works have appeared or are forthcoming in *Constellations*, *Quadrant*, *The Tiger Moth Review*, and *Verandah Journal*.

Njoku Nonso writes from Nigeria. His work, which explores the self as a unit of language, familyhood, spaces, death, grief, and otherness has been published or is forthcoming in *YabaLeft Review*, *Agbowo*, *Bodega*, *20.35 Africa*, *Rising Phoenix Press* (Pushcart-nominated), *Memento: An Anthology of Nigerian Contemporary Poetry*, *Ake Review* and elsewhere. A 2022 Unserious Collective fellow, he's a finalist for Open Drawer Poetry Contest, Lumiere Review Inaugural Writing Contest, and most recently Chestnut Review's Stubborn Writers Contest. He loves stray dogs. Hook up on Twitter: @NN_Emmanuels.

Isibeal Owens is a senior at Rutgers University pursuing her Bachelor's in English. She is originally from Mobile, Alabama, but currently lives in Cape May, New Jersey with her large orange cat. Her work has appeared in *Oyedrum* and *Temenos*.

Kelly Sargent, a Vermont writer and artist, is the author of *Seeing Voices: Poetry in Motion* (2022) and *Lilacs and Teacups* (2022). Her other works, including cover and award-nominated art and poetry, have appeared or are forthcoming in more than sixty literary publications, including *Rattle*, *Newfound*, and *Typehouse Literary Magazine*. She serves as the creative nonfiction editor of *The Bookends Review* and a reviewer for an organization whose mission is to make visible the artistic expression of sexual violence survivors.

Claire Scott is an award-winning poet who has received multiple Pushcart Prize nominations. Her work has appeared in the *Atlanta Review, Bellevue Literary Review, New Ohio Review, Enizagam,* and *Healing Muse,* among others. Claire is the author of *Waiting to be Called* and *Until I Couldn't.* She is the co-author of *Unfolding in Light: A Sisters' Journey in Photography and Poetry.*

Eileen Frankel Tomarchio works as a librarian in a small NJ town. Her writing appears or is forthcoming in *Passages North, The Forge, Longleaf Review, Pithead Chapel, X-R-A-Y, trampset, Flash Frog,* and elsewhere. She holds an MFA from NYU Film. Find her on Twitter @eileentomarchio.

Matina Vossou is a self-taught artist living in Athens, Greece. She uses acrylics and a toothpick, a technique which she learned from her father, who was a naïve painter. Her most recent participations were in Onboards Biennale in Antwerp, Belgium, in Emerging Scene in Dubai, UAE, in Artbox, (Urbanside Gallery in Zurich, Tana Art Place in Venice, Swissartexpo, also in Zurich) and in Expo Metro in the collective artwork, Downtown Los Angeles. She is also included in the 2021 yearbook of the Gran Anuario Internacional de arte contemporáneo, edición Madrid and in ARTISTI '22, Annuario Internazionale d'arte contemporanea, Art Now, Mondadori Store. Besides painting, she also loves writing; her play "The Nothing of People" (a dystopian comedy) was published in Greek in 2018. You can see more of her artwork at: www.instagram.com/matinavossou

Taylor Yingshi is a sophomore at Columbia University making finely detailed, undulating illustrations inspired by a confluence of aesthetics—from the exuberance of Baroque paintings to the granularity of modern digital art. Her work revolves around the preservation and transformation of memory, history, and heritage. Find her on Twitter and Instagram @yingshiart, or at tayloryingshi.com.

Chestnut Review

VOLUME 4   NUMBER 3   WINTER 2023

FOR STUBBORN ARTISTS

COVER ART

Michael Moreth
"Reclining Woman"
Watercolor and pencil, 4 x 6 inches, September 2022

Here is a pencil and watercolor picture I made.
I hope you like it.

Chestnut Review

VOLUME 4 NUMBER 3 WINTER 2023

Chestnut Review LLC, Ithaca, New York
chestnutreview.com

Chestnut Review appears four times a year online, in January, April, July, and October, and once per year in print in July.

ISSN 2688-0350 (online), ISSN 2688-0342 (print)

CONTENTS

Introduction

Winter is a time to look forward to the new year, whether solar or lunar, and turn a new page. We here at *Chestnut Review* are pleased to present the winners of last year's Stubborn Writers Contest in the categories of Fiction, Natalie Harris-Spencer, and Poetry, Max Pasakorn. We also have a new chapbook out, Esperanza Cintrón's *Boulders: Detroit Nature Poems*, which was the finalist of the 2022 Poetry Chapbook Contest. We are in the heart of winter, but we hope these works and our prose and poetry selections will be a salve to the cold sunny days or snowy landscapes that may haunt your windows, a return to emotion and feeling, checking on wellness in search of deeper and more authentic embodiment. Here in North America, many of us have experienced an unprecedented cold snap that has challenged our expectations of place and temperature. For our readers in gentler climates or the global South, we welcome you to the shock of sudden cold and the slow advance of warmth after regaining shelter. In the midst of working on this issue, we will be taking flight, with our Editor-in-Chief and Managing Editor facilitating our first ever retreat in Mexico.

Whether readers, staff, contributors, we are on a journey together, stepping into all the Winter has to offer.

2022 POETRY CHAPBOOK CONTEST FINALIST

Belle Isle

Aunt Myrna lost her cherry and her shoes on Belle Isle
and I hear she wasn't the only one cuz it's a place for firsts
and seconds and slow drives in circles along the shoreline
with kids hanging out of car windows shouting and licking ice
cream cones sans seat belts while their parents blast the radio
or for casting a rod off a long wooden wharf trying to catch fish
you probably shouldn't eat or for games of cricket played by dark
skinned men dressed in white who laugh in island accents or maybe
a quick game of nine holes on a shaggy course or a windblown boat
house wedding with a long silky bride like a Modigliani model drifting
down a winding stream in a canoe followed by a duck squawking at
its trail of ducklings while a hawk circles overhead or you could find
somebody you like and when it gets dark tuck your car into a forested
lane and search for cherries or peaches or lost shoes while deer look
on nose pressed to foggy windows I heard that the island used to be
overrun by snakes so hogs were brought over to get rid of them but
I'm sure they're all gone now cuz it's been a few hundred years

Detroit Salt Mines

Before man, water ruled
churning and becoming
wisps and whirls and
never ending surging like
sound without end until
waves parted and solid
space, hard, unmoving acres
of place revealed ever widening
and washed by a flick, a dizzy twist
of wet that surged and receded
blowing, a breeze, an ocean's
glacial breath quick freezing
eons of ice melting massive
drips drying in sheaths like crumbling
leaves, granules of crusted white
layered hoary grains of lumpy
brackish boulders, miles and miles
of translucent brine collecting
settling, sinking, solidifying
becoming rock becoming clefts
of savory grottos deep below.
Before commerce before roads and cars
before discovery before shafts,
subterranean walls, frosted cascading
paths and tunnels lay like untrampled dew

Praise for *Boulders, Detroit Nature Poems*

Crab grass and dandelions. Verdant rainforests in shattered shops. Raw music of urban life and relentless birdsong. Belle Isle, Eastern Market, Midtown, Cobo and the history of humanity, of capitalism. Absence, presence. The red-eyed nocturnal animal that will not flee your car. Grind and bump of steel, rust, wrecking balls, and yet the turquoise river, its day diamonds. Ah, such song, sensuality, breathless lists and litanies. From the chilling reality of the first poem to the crushing quote from Keynes at the end, this is a body-and-soul rocking, rapping, jiving celebration of the spirit of Detroit. Though there is grief for a lost era, and the natural world has predators whose "absolute power hungers for you." Nature in its stark beauty triumphs everywhere. Cintrón's electric poems will send currents through you. This collection contains a powerful energy, and like Nature itself, becomes vibrant and alive in the hands of this masterful poet.

—Zilka Joseph, author of *In Our Beautiful Bones, Sparrows and Dust, Sharp Blue Search of Flame*

Esperanza Cintrón's *Boulders* is a celebratory lyric examining the rich beauty of Detroit. The city's cold, its spring, its island and its birds all make appearances in this collection where the city's natural landscape is a lively character overtaking abandoned buildings and threatening to cross the threshold of houses. Cintrón's lush images and stunning sounds cascade throughout the book building an unforgettable love song dedicated to the history and the present of post-industrial Detroit.

—Nandi Comer, author of *Tapping Out*

Esperanza Cintrón is the Pushcart-nominated author of *Shades, Detroit Love Stories*, a 2020 Michigan Notable Book, published by Wayne State University Press. She has three books of poetry: *Visions of a Post-Apocalyptic Sunrise*, the Naomi Long Madgett Award winner *What Keeps Me Sane*, and *Chocolate City Latina*. She was a Callaloo Writing Fellow at Brown and Oxford Universities, recipient of a Michigan Council for the Arts Individual Artist Grant and a NEH educator's scholarship, and has a doctorate in English literature from the State University of New York at Albany. Under the nom de plume Alegra Verde, she has written several short works of fiction, many of which have been translated into various languages.

Chestnut Review
CHAPBOOKS

2022 CHESTNUT REVIEW CHAPBOOK CONTEST FINALIST

Boulders

Detroit Nature Poems

Esperanza Cintrón

MARIA S. PICONE

A Conversation with Esperanza Cintrón, Poetry Chapbook Finalist

NB: This conversation has been truncated and is available in full on our website; tune in for much more content and discussion of Esperanza's chapbook and her work as a poet and activist.

MP: Welcome! I'm here with Esperanza Cintrón, the author of the new CR chapbook Boulders and the runner-up of our 2022 Poetry Chapbook Contest. Esperanza, we absolutely love your poetry! Your work immediately grabbed me by the throat from the beginning and there's a strong artistic imagining from the title Boulders: Detroit Nature Poems and the excerpt from A Divertimento for Rocks that starts off the collection. So, clearly you had a strong artistic vision going into this chapbook—can you tell us a bit about where that came from and what the genesis of that was like?

EC: It's sort of freeform—I got this idea (which is in the blurb at the beginning) that I'm in Michigan, a very nature-oriented state, with mountains, farms and so forth and then you've got Detroit, so, it's like, we get a lot of nature-oriented poetry but not a lot of Detroit nature. We've got nature! We've got birds, trees, and I wanted to capture this, because you think of city and industry and the Renaissance Building, but we're a very diverse city in terms of our ecological, geological aspects. That's what I went into and the poems just started coming.

MP: I really think this is an ecological chapbook for today, for exactly that reason. When we think of cities we think of man-made, artificial constructs but, as we've seen with the climate crisis and the COVID pandemic and other things, we're encroaching on nature, nature is encroaching on us, and we share and embody the same space. One thing that drew me to your chapbook was—not an exact quote, but Aimee Nezhukumatathil said that BIPOC poets aren't thought of as ecological writers because they're just associated with cities, especially the inner city,

EC: Right? Like we don't care about the climate? About living?

MP: Yes! I see this false dichotomy all the time: this noble, generally white poet or writer in nature, like a Rachel Carson or a Henry Thoreau, the lone figure away from civilization picking out something about man, and these BIPOC people telling these stories, but it has nothing to do with nature, and I like the way this [chapbook] melds this urban landscape that's ecological, geologi-cal, intensely human and brimming with this experience.

EC: That's really what I was trying to capture. We as human beings are part of that whole thing. In Detroit we lost so much of the actual buildings—a lot of stuff was razed and torn down because we didn't have the money to keep it up so part of the land did go feral, if you will—it started to forest, to grow in the city. I grew up in a city that of one and a half million people and we were number one in individual homeowners so there were all these beautiful brick homes and all these plots. Now if you go there, whole blocks have been razed, and the city, because it's been gentrified, is keeping the grass cut low, but there used to be little forests, and you could go down the block and see trees that had sprouted, and all kinds of growth. I mention these types of growth in my chapbook like crabgrass and all kinds of other things that actually took over the city. To me, that's phenomenal, that Mother Nature, God, the spirits, the powers all said "Hey! I'm going to let my other children, plants and animals, do what they do." It made me begin to understand how little we are. How little we mean in the scheme of things. It's probably Nostradamus-like but I don't mean it that way. I mean that we should wake up and recognize that we have to coexist.

MP: I love that—that's exactly what I see in these poems—a crowdedness, but it's alive, and we're so small, but then everything else is raised to that level: the crabgrass and us. We are on this equal playing field in this Detroit landscape. A polyphony of characters with an urban focus, but some of the characters are natural things.

EC: One of my favorite characters in my poetry is the possum that's staring me down—it represents all that is nature. It's like, "Really? I'm here too" and it's based on a real thing that happened because it's dark, not a lot of streetlights, but I could see that possum's red eyes. I'm sitting in a car, all that steel around me, and I'm still scared of that possum because that possum just seemed to have some power that I needed to respect.

MP: I love how this collection takes us through that lens, defamiliarizing things in a powerful way, and we as readers have to give respect to nature, the landscape we're embedded in, the moment we're living in now and that's what's wonderful about this chapbook.

A lot of these poems are written in what we might call a breathless style, a new type of form that you've created: medium-length lines, one stanza, very minimal punctuation and almost no end stops. This goes to that symphony of characters—to me there's an orchestration to these poems. Is that a technique that you honed for this chapbook specifically or is it something that characterizes a lot of your poetry?

EC: It's a progression—my earlier poems were more traditional or standard, but it's become more and more loose like this but for Boulders, the white space or line breaks are supposed to be the punctuation. That's where you as a reader are meant to take your breath. If you don't get a breath then, you're just out of luck. I wanted to let the poems create their own rhythm. A lot of them I wrote many times and did different line breaks until I felt like the poem and the thing that needed to be said was said in its own rhythm. I had a really difficult time with the salt mines— I rewrote that poem so many times trying to get the sense of evolution.

MP: There's so much there, right?

EC: Yes, even in the concept of how that salt formed from liquid. I was trying to speak to that sense of evolution, formation, geology as biology.

MP: There's so many specific words to hold onto, to that idea of a whirlpool that is so much stronger and more powerful, and also more important than you.

EC: I have to thank you though, Maria, because your notes about the ending helped me to heighten it. It's hard to know where to end because that's a continuous process. Right now, men are down there mining this salt and selling it, but that's only another part of the process, because eventually that will change, and I don't know whether, with all our climate situations—earthquakes, all kinds of other ecological things that could shift—I don't know what the next step is, but I was trying to get to the sense that this was just one step in the evolution of this piece of rock.

MP: Thank you so much for talking with me today. It was hilarious, and I'm so looking forward to seeing your chapbook in physical form in my hands and getting it out there in the world.

EC: Thank you for understanding. You made me feel like I achieved what I was trying to do, so thank you very much, Maria.

MP: Thank you so much! But I don't think that has anything to do with me. I think that with the strength of the work, everybody's going to see it.

Cover Art (right) by Julian Wong

Guāi Guāi

On Sunday afternoons, after church, Mama and Baba take us to 99 Ranch. They've been going to this Asian grocery store, I don't know, probably since they left Taiwan and came to the United States.

Today, I don't want to go.

My toes hurt from the new shoes Mama wanted me to wear for church. They look like doll shoes: white and round, with a Velcro strap across the foot. I wasn't sure how to feel about them, but when I put them on, Mama smiled in that proud way, the way she did when I won the Bible verse memorization contest and beat Irene, the star student in my Sunday school class. So I'm wearing them. They didn't hurt right away, but now my pinky toes are squished.

I just want to go home. But Mama and Ollie are only two steps away from the entrance and Baba is already telling Derek to grab a cart, so I don't say anything.

The sliding doors open. Our shopping cart rattles over the metal threshold, and a rainbow sea of fruits and vegetables greets us. My shoes squeak on the linoleum floor. The supermarket smells like dirt, like the bitter Chinese medicine that Mama makes us drink when we're sick, and like the beach. Mama and Baba join all the other Asian moms and dads to go look for whatever they look for. They leave me and my two brothers in the only area that we care about in the whole store: the snack aisle.

For a moment, I forget about my shoes. Colorful packets of round, juicy gummies catch my eye: kiwi, muscat (I think that means grape), lychee, peach, and apple flavors lined up in a row. A tall, skinny boy walks past me and reaches for a bag of shrimp chips on a high shelf. Further down the aisle, two girls hold a box of Choco Pies, mini chocolate-covered cakes with a creamy marshmallow filling. Across from them, a little boy about Ollie's height hugs a bag of milky White Rabbit candies wrapped in rice paper.

My mouth waters. I could spend a whole day in this aisle, looking through each row. But there are so many other kids without their parents here, bad and noisy, getting in the way. They pick up bags, crumple them, and put them back in the wrong places. Mama would yell at me if I did that. I'm getting annoyed because we don't have much time; Derek, Ollie, and I each get to put only one snack in the cart—that's always the rule—and we have to decide before Mama and Baba finish their shopping.

Derek is annoyed, too. He has that look on his face, the scary one that lets you know you shouldn't mess with him. Taller and older than the rest of us, he pushes his way through the crowd. Some glare at him but are too afraid to do anything else. I trail behind, excusing myself each time I squeeze past someone, the way Mama taught me. Ollie holds on to me, his sweaty little hand in mine.

When we get to Derek, he's already made his choice: a Taiwanese corn puff snack in a lime green bag called Guāi Guāi (乖乖). It's Chinese for "(be) good," or "obedient." Mama said it to me this morning when I was putting on my shoes. *Guāi guāi, listen to Mama.* I think it's kind of funny that Derek got this because he listens to loud rap music with bad words and is getting a C in math and is definitely not guāi.

But the snack is really good: crunchy, sweet, and addicting.

There's even a toy in the bag and it's a surprise every time. Everybody likes it in my Sunday school class; it's one of the best prizes we can get by redeeming the stickers we earn for reading Bible stories. Last time, I saved up fifteen stickers for three whole bags. I was so proud of myself, until Mama told me that Irene had two more stickers than me and that I should be reading more. I don't really like Irene.

Ollie tugs on my hand. He's found some chips with a yellow Pikachu on the bag. I have no idea what flavor they are, so he probably doesn't know either; I bet he just grabbed them because he's obsessed with watching Pokémon right now. But I don't have time to tell him to pick something else because I'm still torn between the cookies-and-cream Pocky and the strawberry Yan Yan when I hear Baba's voice yell out, "Kids, we're checking out!"

I quickly place both of them back on the shelf—in their original places—and grab a box of chocolate-filled Koala's March cookies instead. Ollie will probably like these, too; maybe I'll let him have some. I look around, and Derek is nowhere to be seen. Stupid Derek. He never waits for us. He's probably already sprinted to the register and slam-dunked his Guāi Guāi into the cart. So I start running, pulling Ollie along behind me because he's so slow and will never make it before Baba starts paying, faster and faster, my feet hurt but it doesn't matter, we're almost there, I turn the corner, and bam! I crash into a shopping cart.

On the other side of the cart is a lady with a neat hair bun, reaching toward a delicately balanced tower of tomatoes. The cart's handle shoves into her back, propelling her forward, and I watch in horror as the tower collapses. A wave of tomatoes tumble to the floor, fast and eager, like Derek and his wild friends jumping into a pool on a summer day, splashing water everywhere.

Ollie is sprawled out on the floor next to me, still clutching his chips. Somehow, I still have my koala cookies, too. My right shoe has a dark smudge from where it dragged, and my left shoulder throbs.

I look up. Mama, the lady with the cart, and a store worker are all there. Tomatoes surround us.

The other Asian moms and dads have stopped what they're doing, gawking, murmuring to each other and shaking their heads. I feel like a zoo animal, and I want to hide behind Mama. But Mama is a flapping bird, flitting here, picking up tomatoes there, saying sorry, sorry a hundred times in Chinese to the shopping cart lady and the worker. The worker is annoyed. She sighs and wags her finger. But the lady that I crashed into is nicer. She pats me on the head and says to Mama, it's OK, she has two boys at home, she knows how kids can be. Then she says with a smile, like she is making a joke, that she'd heard girls were less wild, but it looks like maybe not!

The lady tousles my hair and laughs. I frown and smooth it back down with my hands. The joke wasn't funny, because I'm not wild. I'm not like the other kids in the snack aisle. I'm not like Derek. And all the other moms and dads are still watching. Maybe some of them even go to our church. Mama gives the lady a tight-lipped smile, but her face turns the color of the tomatoes.

She drags me and Ollie to the register, where Baba and Derek are waiting for us. Baba takes Ollie's Pikachu chips and drops them on the belt behind Derek's snack. I reach to give my chocolate koalas to Baba, but Mama snatches them out of my hand. She flings them to the side, and they land in a pile of mooncakes where they don't belong.

Chén Xiǎotíng, she says, emphasizing each syllable. How many times has she told me not to run in the store? Why won't I behave? Why won't I listen to her? Mama rarely says my Chi-

nese name, so I should be scared, but I can't take my eyes off
the koalas, discarded and abandoned, and all I feel is anger and
confusion.

I did listen to her. I behaved, not like all the other kids. Ol-
lie was just too slow, we wouldn't have made it in time—I want
to say all these things, and more, but tears spring to my eyes and
what escapes my mouth is a wild cry: Derek ran, too, I just know
he did, how come only I'm getting punished.

Before I can say anything else, Mama says she doesn't want
to hear it, I should know better, I'm setting a bad example, Ol-
lie and I could have been hurt, and yes, maybe Derek ran, too,
but well, boys will be boys, she expected more from me, girls
can't behave like this. She keeps going. Didn't I hear that lady
call me wild, now my new shoes are dirty, she just bought them
last week, how is she going to show her face in this market or at
church again, and why couldn't I just be more like Irene who sits
still and gets straight A's and is guāi?

At this, Baba puts his hand on Mama's arm. He looks like he's
about to say something, but then Ollie pulls at his leg and he
turns away from her. Derek stands next to the shopping cart, still
and quiet, as if he doesn't have a part in all of this.

In the parking lot, I climb into the last row of the car. Derek
sits in the middle row next to Ollie and rips open his bag of Guāi
Guāi. The sweet fragrance reaches my nostrils. His loud crunches
grate on my ears as he gobbles up the whole bag without sharing
a single one. Ollie eats two of his mystery chips, makes a face,
and dumps the rest out on the floor.

Tears stream down my face, snot forming in my nose. I sniff,
softly at first, then hard, and the mucus travels back up and re-
surfaces in my mouth. I swallow. It isn't until after we get home,
after I take off my painful shoes, after I go to my room and
finally stop crying, that I wonder: will I be guāi if I just don't run

and keep my shoes clean and listen to Mama, or are there more
rules that I don't know, because I get straight A's, too.

STEVE DENEHAN

"Yachts on Fire"
Oil on canvas, 16 x 12 inches, March 2018
(Next Page)

Philemaphobia or the Fear of Kissing

A fear of pimples, of dander, of losing my voice
around boys, of rumpled blouses, unfurling hems,

buttons missing or undone. I am afraid of
backseats. Uneasy in upswept hair, with bobby pins &

clips, the slow unrolling of curls. Scared of underarm hair,
curly, unsightly, unevenly shaved. Afraid of

dark alleys without stars. The intrusion of
deft hands beneath my shirt. Not knowing

exactly how to position my mouth. The sharp
exquisite bite of braces. The size of the pores on my

face. The feeling I get when his hand wrestles in
folds of my skirt. Because my life's a great

galaxy of mistakes and this may be one more, his eyes
glazed over, breath stopped in his throat. Because fat

hips, wide thighs, upper arms that jiggle. Because I can't
help thinking about garlic, tuna fish, and what might still be stuck

inside his mouth. Because I practiced in a mirror and still can't get
it right. Because lipstick smears. Because I can barely move in tight

jeans. In my room, I tear apart my closet, grab hangers,
juggle jerseys, side-slit skirts, fuchsia & black. Afraid to sit on a boy's

knees, feel his long bones, foreign & fragile, his fingers stiff as piano
keys, broken pieces of song. Because a pocketed bird always

longs for escape. In his throat, a tumble of germs, unnamed,
last vestige of some unnatural disease. In my mouth,

my tongue presses against the bench of my teeth. Each
morning I brush them, tie fractious hair back on my soft-shelled

neck, recite remedies for heartbreak, words without rhymes,
names of various cloud formations that signal rain.

Open your lips and next it's your legs, your ribs, the dark
outside of your heart, and you're spilling singed marrow on

parchment pages, leading him between fence slats, to the
puzzle of your room. I don't know what it takes. I've failed quiz after

quiz in chemistry, equations tumbling in my eyes before I
quit trying, turn over the paper, pretend I have all the answers. I can't

reveal how little there is inside—pebbles, a clutch of empty eggs,
rose stems, broken and bleeding. Because I'm afraid when he

slips his hand down my satin sleeve, he will feel the slickness of
sheets in the weave, will feel heat rising from me. I fear

trodden paths, ways already taken, footprints encased in mud,
taut mouths, and secret loves. What I believe about myself—once

undone—will spin apart, drift into nebulas of longing, the charred
underside of stars, like motes of a hymn splintered, lodged in

veins and arteries. Because my wings, in salt-tinged air,
vivid with glint of feathers, are too easily crushed. Because I

worry about how it will look, how it may lead to days,
weeks of trembling, of uncertainty. Because I

excite too easily. Afraid of needles, heights, open air,
x-rays that will expose my missing bones. If I say

yes, I open the door. I am so tired of being alone
year after year. So afraid of having my heart

zipped and bagged. Because if I enter this perilous
zone, how will I find the map, how will I chart my course?

SHARON LIN

Common Flower Parts

Ying Ying told us secrets in the girl's bathroom like how, when we turned ten, our bodies bloomed. She proved it by plucking a petal from between her legs, a sliver of pink dotted red. That's the thing about blooming, she said, you bloom inside out. We felt between our legs for the edge of a flower, but felt only stumps. Ying Ying said that sometimes the flower was harder to find, like her mum's, which she could only find with a mirror pressed up to her bum. I asked her what kind of mirror and she laughed at me. I went home to the bathroom with the mirror that stretches from the ceiling to the floor and pulled myself onto the toilet, facing the reflecting wall. Between my legs, I saw a bud and was suddenly afraid of thorns. Ma kept scissors in the cabinet for cutting dress tags and splinters, so I fetched them. I locked the door. I was afraid the flower might leak, so I covered the bathroom tiles in toilet paper, then sat and opened my legs. We learned about flowers in science class when Mrs. Jones showed us a chart of common flower parts. The ovary turns into a stigma, surrounded by petals. I got a 110 on the test because I remembered to separate the pistil from the stamens. But where did the flower turn into a stem? I pulled away from the flower, afraid again. When my sister was born, she was attached to a stem. I stood beside Ma, my head just over the hospital bed. The doctor withdrew himself, arms retreating from under the sheets. His wrists glistened, curled with strands of vines and thorns.

But I didn't see vines inside me, nor thorns. I placed the scissors
on the floor then reached two fingers back towards the stamen,
past the pistil, until I found the stem. I withdrew my hand. There
were no petals between my fingers, but white nectar-coated
seeds. When I placed them in mouth, they tasted like mango-
steens, strong and sweet.

S A M U E L   A D E Y E M I

November Ends

It is harmattan again. The people I love, like
the old trees, are distant or dying. I walk the
boulevards outside the house. The air, sharp,
whitened by a dry cold. There is a loneliness
inside the morning breeze. I can tell because
it reaches for my wrists, wants to sit on skin
like mist upon a hill. It is the same wet thing
that weathers me. It clouds, quietly, inside a
place I cannot name. Such territory, the body.
Often we seem to be visitors within its walls.
As in, who knew you could hurt like that, little
heart? Anyway, someone else has to teach the
wind not to be lonely. I have been preoccupied,
learning what to do with the multitude of myself.
I am thinking of less harmful ways to be alone.
So far, the plot is going terribly bad. Even the
music is some kind of knife. It doesn't wound,
but it unwinds the wound. I know one thing is
certain—I do not deserve my sadness. Forget
the theory that the humble would never proclaim
their humility. I am a good man. But we must
be foolish if we think, just for our goodness,
the world must offer us any mercy. The wine
that poisons the ghoul will poison the saint.
And I think, in spite of the bluntness, it is fair.

POETRY: FIRST PLACE

เข้าใจ (kaojai) // to understand, lit. to enter the heart (n.)

1. On 19 September 2028, Max receives a passport from Singapore. The passport is red. It shows a lion and tiger presenting a Singapore crest. The way the two felines longingly gaze forward with their paws gripping the placard reminds Max of the afternoon-long prize-giving ceremonies that they attended. Max had a lot of trouble putting on ties as a 10-year-old. When Max wants to travel, they retrieve the newly minted book from their dresser, where they also keep their underused eyeshadow palettes. Before leaving, Max would flip to the first page to ensure that their face still looks the as same the profile photo taken years before, with their windswept hair shiny, their cheeks plump and red-ripe, and their lips slightly curved in an awkward smile. Once, they were a bit self-conscious when the airport staff said, with an undertone of dread, that they've slimmed down, as if Max was already partway out of this world. Max knew the staff did not mean any malice, but they wanted to ensure that anyone who wanted to see them and befriend them could see them for who they were.

2. On 5 April 2018, Max learns the makeup technique known as the contour. Not to be confused with the corset, the contour allows Max to add a shadow beneath their cheeks, to give the illusion that their face is sculpted like a Greek statue. Max does not really want to be associated with Greek statues and their deliberately small penises, but they like how the made-believe shadows appeared to embrace their cheeks with a beautiful flesh-tone colour. To contour, Max would use a specific brush that is shaped like a shark's tooth to apply a rich brown powder, swiping downwards and blending out, an elegant darkness radiating from an imaginary hollow. Max seems to find themselves physically existing in that space, like an in-between stage of sinking and soaring. Going nowhere but having a clear direction. Soon, Max would be fascinated with colour again. But, for those short days, Max would find themselves immersed in a body of contrasts.

3. On 26 January 2042, Max discovers they have a long-lost twin who migrated to an English-speaking country in his childhood. When Max met him for dinner at a decently pricey Middle East-ern restaurant, Max did not realise the similarities they shared. Despite being identical, he looks nothing like Max. He is about the same height, but stood taller, broad-backed and broad-chest-ed. He got his teeth fixed so he has a beautiful smile he describes as a "lady killer." He has a Southeast Asian wife and fathered two beautiful girls from an emotional distance as a computer engi-neer. He tells Max he wasn't particular good at Math in school, but he found this guy who hooked him up with his first job and he has been posting on LinkedIn so he has a somewhat decent career. He is wearing a bomber jacket, white shirt, and tapered jeans, as if he went to an American high school in the '50s and never graduated. His beard grows scruffily around the curvature of his face. Max tells him he never thought the DNA bestowed

upon him could have created a human so suited for life in this social planet. They were wrong. The man eats his food slowly, watching Max with a curious gaze as the conversation unfolded, their lives splaying themselves out like a road map of missed opportunities. Max tells him that they live in a small apartment with their masculine-presenting partner about 5km from the ocean. After that night, the two would trade numbers but never speak to each other again.

4. On 10 November 2082, Max would die, surrounded by flowers that would wilt soon after, in a hospital that was not particularly accessible to the people who cared about them. When Max heaves their last breath, the strongest memory that resurfaced was them dancing to a Dua Lipa song in a giant ballroom, their arms wrapped around their partner as their feet moved, unco-ordinated, like flat-footed penguins. Behind them, the disco lights painted the ceiling in a ceremonious rainbow as the music crescendoed to a pause. They kissed. Max remembers the softness of their partner's lips, pressed against theirs, nerve endings smooshed into connectivity like the plugs of a computer. It was probably the sensations of surprise that made Max cherish this memory so dearly. The funeral would be a much sadder occasion. The undertaker would use her delicate fingers to twist Max's lips into a smile, a pretense that Max was happy when they passed on. But Max doesn't mind. There are worse things to lie about.

5. On 6 February 2090, Max's last book is published. It does so badly at the bookstores that the publisher goes bankrupt. Ten years later, a literary critic researching queer literature from the 21st century picks it up and writes a review that makes the book spike in popularity. A larger, more established press reprints the book and earns enough profit to start a literary charity dedicated

to developing more queer writers. But they don't. The money is stored digitally in a corporate bank account.

6. On 21 July 1995, Max formed in their mother's stomach. They don't remember much of this moment, obviously, but they would later find out from their mother that the doctor thought they were a girl in the womb, because the ultrascan couldn't detect the penis. As a housewarming gift, their parents bought them a pink blanket into their childhood crib, in a room that would soon be decorated with cheap stickers bought from a nearby market. Max was always very kind to their mother. Her womb, having suffered two miscarriages, must not have been the most comfortable. Apparently, Max would kick much less than other fetuses, as if preserving the passage that allowed them to enter this world. When Max heaved their first breath after the C-Section, they had the cry of any regular baby born to middle-aged parents. Uwah, uwah. Max's parents probably believed their child was normal then. As normal as any other children in the infirmary were.

FICTION: FIRST PLACE

Fish Mother

I kill the biggest koi within two days of moving into the crooked house. I know it's dead because it's lying on its side like an offering, one globular eye stretched taut, gazing up. The remaining koi and orfe family sink to the bottom and stay there for three days. Like they're in mourning.

The fish come with the house. A package deal, the pushy realtor tells us. I like the American house, its suburban location, my husband's inheritance allowing us more square footage than we ever would have believed possible, even though it looks like it's leaning slightly to the left.

Is it just me, or is it crooked? I ask.

It's just you.

I really wish it didn't have that koi pond. A pond is a lot of work, I say. Are you sure we're up to it?

We are, my husband assures me, kissing the bone above my eyebrow.

We're ready. It's time. These things come in the customary order: 1. Get married. 2. Buy a house. 3. Settle down. This is what we signed up for, isn't it? Weren't we both in on it, this spousal pact? Who can argue it, now?

I picture the fat, dead fish—J. Edgar—as I'm lying on the oh-bee bed, the paper-thin salmon gown split open at the front, a disposable sheet on my lap (for modesty), feet balancing in hospital stirrups.

Are you one hundred percent sure you want your IUD removed today? she asks. We can always pop in another.

Five-to-seven years of no periods, no babies, no responsibilities. Thank you, Mirena. Pop in another? It would be my third. Can we keep kicking the inevitable can down the road?

Is anyone ever one hundred percent, I joke, but she doesn't smile. Probability isn't funny. Yes, I confirm. Yes, I'm sure.

My poor J. Edgar, thick and fleshy: dead by over-indulgence, by my hand. I sprinkled one too many orange pyramid crackers and he hoovered them all, the greedy imp. I *told* my husband we didn't know how to look after koi. That this was a terrible idea. That we should have sold them on Ebay. J. Edgar, his belly bobbing, unresponsive to the prods from the fishing net stick.

Pri? What are you doing? He's dead. You overfed him.

Did I? is all I can manage. Did I?

Oh, J. I fish him out, slop him on to the deck, and wrestle him into a garbage bag for the next morning's collection, tears hurtling down my cheeks. He didn't deserve to die like this. Who am I kidding? I can't even look after a basic house plant. I consistently overwater, saturating the soil until it turns a blue-black. The aloe vera plant is only supposed to be watered once a month, its prickly sage leaves more than capable of flourishing on the windowsill. But I can't help myself. Water flows. I'm a homeowner now. There's much to be done.

I'm sorry, Priyanka, says the oh-bee, in a serious sort of way. I'm afraid I can't see the strings. It's likely they've curled up inside you. Are you okay just waiting there for a minute? I need to get up into your uterus. Let me see if I can find a thinner instrument. Hold, please.

Am I okay? My legs are butterflied. Inside me: vanishing

strings, like a magic trick. Ta-da! I hold, please. The coil has been inside me for so long that it's become a part of me. It's a long-standing comfort between my husband and me. No babies! No periods! What a joy to have this plasticky, t-shaped friend stuck up there, lodged in, keeping us both safe. What pure joy, to not have to rely on other, more awkward forms of contraception. Cheers to you, Mirena. You've been a champ.

She's back. Here we go, she soothes. Just breathe.

The pain is electric and precise. Panic seizes. I lick my lips; my lipstick is cold and grainy under my tongue. I tap my fingers, playing a soundless piano on the top of my gown.

Breathe, breathe. There we go.

Gotcha! she exclaims, like she's won a soft plush toy from a carnival claw machine, and she's showing it to me, its presence eerie and unreal. There, it's out, banished from my body, the two strings dangling in afterthought. On one arm, watery blood clings. Before I can conjure up a suitable goodbye, it is gone.

That was a stubborn one, she tuts.

She shows me the length of the instrument, how it curves ever so slightly at one end, the contraption pinching. I regard it in disbelief. The things we women go through.

You're all set. Just remember to keep taking your prenatals. Book a follow-up if you don't have a period in two months. Good luck!

And I'm fumbling into my clothes, the cramps alien, my body bending and reacting to the invasion, and all I can think is: this is it, we're doing this, it's all over, it's on.

***

It's been three weeks since the oh-bee visit. Ibuprofen fixes the cramps. The prenatal vitamins leave a lingering taste of cod liver oil. I wander from room to room, out to the deck, to the yard, unpacking boxes, wall-mounting photo frames, feeding the fish. I invent names for the rest of them: I dub the red one Red Dead, the black and white one Cow Splotch, the silvery, almost see-through one Gray Beard. There are others. More. I can't see them all. The water's too thick, and they're too fast: a flash of orange, a roar of red. I switch off the bubbler in an attempt to get them to rise to the surface, claiming oxygen. The fish freak, slapping and plopping, creating a lather. I switch it back on again. They sink, vibrating beneath the surface of the water, refusing to play ball.

It is a fat, burning summer, loaded with electric storms, which means that the fish should, in theory, be super active, spurred on by the frequent rain showers, their lips popping at the bubbles, investigating the rain, kissing up. But they aren't prepared to show themselves to me, not after what I did to J. Edgar. I'm determined to win back their trust.

Hey little fishies, I sing, as I sprinkle the foul-smelling graze. Where are you? I'm doing everything in my power to entice them. No dice. The smell of fish food clings to my fingers.

Give me a chance, I want to scream. I can be a good mother to you!

I google "how long do koi live" and discover it's fucking ages, even longer than the total amount of time I've been married, although I am encouraged to learn that they take a seasonal hiatus, hibernating at the bottom against the winter freeze, buried under slow flurries that settle on diamond-hard ice, kept alive only by an electric heated ring. But that's at least four months away. For now, as elusive as they are, they are active. And they hate me.

I order a pond testing kit from Amazon Prime that arrives the next day. I dip test tubes into the murky water, measuring the alkaline on a scale of forest-green to lilac to lemon. The results are bad. Really, really bad.

Hey, love, I call. We're going to have to change the pond water. Or more of them are going to die.

What's the problem? I thought you overfed the white one?

It's the water, this time. Not the fish food. Can you give me a hand?

Busy.

He empties himself in a fast shrug, and I realize that I'm talking to the back of the house, and not my husband.

***

It's been two months, and no period. I take a test. It's negative. I book an appointment for blood work.

My husband has never been one to overanalyze. Just give it time, he says. You're putting too much pressure on it. Relax, honey.

I sit on the deck for hours, a gripping page-turner on my lap. I don't read. Instead, I watch their every fishy move. Not counting J. Edgar, R.I.P., there are fourteen koi and five golden orfe. They slide and swish and bubble, little flashes of brilliance, their fins as thin as feathers. Bloodless. Aimless. They infuriate me. They answer to no one. They swim without fear. God, I envy them. The book I'm attempting to read—a New York Times Bestseller—is a *Pride and Prejudice* retelling. I'm not even halfway in, and I'm so mad at the characters. Mad at all that time wasted. My heart heaves with the loss.

The crooked house is too big for just two people. Its grandness—at first dreamy and alluring—is now overbearing. It's a four-bedroom colonial, off-center and massive, with a heated driveway, Hansel and Gretel-style shutters with heart stencils, and landscaped gardens. And, oh, how perfect: a fucking koi pond. A *koi pond*. The space is obscene. How can just two people live here? My husband tells me that this is the American dream, that we should be grateful for our specific circumstance. We are blessed.

You're selfish, I whisper to his back, in bed, and I don't mean about the big, empty house. I mean that he's selfish to expect me to look after all those fish. What did he think would happen? He *let* me kill J. Edgar. Okay, so he didn't put the extra fish food in my hand, but he *knows* that I have a propensity to overfeed things. Why didn't he stop me? I pull down my SLEEPING BITCHY eye shades, the ones I got for White Elephant gift exchange last year, and turn my back. I rarely make it all the way through the night; the shades slip up against my hairline like a sweat band. I blink into the quietness of the bedroom, the alarm clock flashing five, always five. Five, five, five. Five to this. Five after that. Nearly. Not quite the hour.

My body is a war zone: dodging, firing, sheltering. I'm grossed out by what's coming, this change. Disgusted. Shouldn't he be more scared? Doesn't he realize we're altering things beyond repair? No. He is calm, as always. Bastard. He cradles me in his arms, as always. He holds me close. As fucking always.

I wake to the wet embers of another summer storm. The gutters are brimming with it. I look out the bedroom window, and spy something on the garage roof below—a rat?—no, bigger than a rat. Whiter than a rat's fuzz. Shinier. It's amphibian.

It is Gray Beard.

I scream at the decapitated koi, a crimson ring where its face used to be.

What? What's happened? Are you okay? My husband rushes in, a fuzzy bath towel wrapped around his perfect waist.

I smother my mouth and point.

The fuck?

I run away from him, bounding downstairs, my throat ablaze. The ends of my slippers grow wetter on the deck, the bottoms of my pajamas soaking. He follows.

Shit. I'm sorry, baby. It was probably an owl or a hawk, he says from behind me, in his perfect, soothing voice. Or maybe even a racoon; those little shits can climb. That's the only way it got up there. Don't worry, honey. We'll get a net to cover the surface, to stop it happening again. He pauses, then adds: At least it didn't leave any marks on the deck.

I count ten. There are ten fish left. From nineteen (not including J. Edgar, rest his soul). Nine dead. It's a massacre. A bloody massacre. Cramps seize my womb. From the angle I'm standing, my husband is too close to the water's edge, his stance taut and edgy. The exterior of the house is more than just crooked, I realize; it's *insane*, totally lopsided, as if it isn't touching the earth, the very foundations it was built upon.

Get away from there! I sob. Get back.

My babies are dead. I collapse to my knees. I'm in mourning.

Red Dead slips across the water's surface, his scales a dark, meaty crimson in the early sunshine, and from miles and miles inside me, I feel something glide and stir.

Seascape

Color photograph, 16 x 9 inches, Hancock Co, Maine, October 2021
(Next Page)

Recurrence

Peering into the scoured bathtub, I spot
sour mildew budding. I wake to pink biofilm
on graying porcelain. Even slime mold has memory;
its amoeba body retrieves oat flakes. After I scythe
seven inches of hair, still I feel long strands running
down my spine. Ever since the flood, I try not to hold
onto much, exfoliate dead cells as if this excess
might weigh down a life raft. I slip pale sea glass
into my pocket only to part with it once I reach the car.
I used to capture wild hermit crabs, place them
in salted tap water, swooshing the tupperware
to mimic waves. I thought I could trick them
into being home. The hermit crabs lasted a day,
leaving behind their tiny calcified capsules, perfect
like piped frosting. The brain wants to be buoyant,
shedding ghosts to avoid overgrowth. We're meant
to slough off the past, but I still don't know
where to keep the shells the tide gives back.

KATIE KEMPLE

Recycling died, like Santa and God.

A lifetime of plastic bottles and the notes I'd left,
all in the Pacific garbage patch, a triangle
of patriarchal green, the arrows a circle-jerk.
My love letter to the earth, laughed at.
Santa's a kind of consumer god drinking a Coke.
He brought us plastics to fill our throats. Even
the school play used plastic particles in place
of snow. And it was beautiful. Santa took his
synthetic beard off, and I prepared to become
an adult in the church. For confirmation,
I attended the mass of the unborn children.
But if heaven before life, why not joy for a soul
to arrive back home with God? That's recycling.
Men in long dresses talked about the host,
the Holy Ghost, and the Virgin Mary. Women
were Coke machines. And that was the perfect
scheme. Body coin-opping new disposable life.

ALISON LUBAR

Self Portrait in a Type of Mirror

We sketch each other, sit knee-to-knee.
I am six. My mother is still post-partum,

another loss. I am once again an only
child. I know faces are circles. A neck

is a rectangle. Use the side of the pencil
for thick hair. The point makes tiny wisps.

Leave a white oval in the pupil– to imitate
cartoons. Everything looks better in my head.

On paper, she smiles, close-lipped, a little
fallen comma at each corner. No wrinkles

because I love her today. I know it's bad.
I know she'll say it's great. She uses

charcoal. I never realized she gave me
eyelashes, too. Now, they're here forever.

I am always this small and pretty, to her. All
in black and white. Everything greyscale.

Eyes are already rounded like teardrops.
Her basement art room is chilly for Spring,

and I can bear only ten minutes until I have
to crawl into her lap. I am too young to know

the heart has no easy shape.

Palomita Azul

The man who put the baby in me tried to get me to end the pregnancy. Even though this was against the rules, he could make it possible. It was a mistake, I pleaded. You were stupid, he said.

When I refused, he cut off all contact. Those are not the rules, he said this time. It was as though the year we spent as lovers had never happened.

At first, I did not leave my small one-bedroom apartment in Cambridge to avoid having my pregnancy detected. My job as a researcher didn't require me to go to the office, and I'd be able to hide my condition from my coworkers by being careful that the camera only showed me from the shoulders up during virtual meetings.

I thought if I had the baby at home without anyone knowing, I could take it with me, somewhere else, anyplace else. Then I started to make plans to leave. But the man had reported my pregnancy to the system. Medical care was arranged for me, and I was visited regularly by a nurse. She was about my age, quiet, with pale skin and hair the color of straw.

The nurse locked a bracelet to my wrist and gave me a packet of information that I put aside without reading. When I asked if there was any way I would be allowed to keep the baby, she said nothing and pointed to the packet. What will happen to him, I said. He will be cared for, she said, and went back to saying nothing.

After she left, I flipped through the packet. More rules, including information about the birth quota, established by the Leader after the last sickness, which had wiped out nearly half the population. Only whites who could offer proof of their pure ancestry had no limits to the number of children they could have.

Genetic tests had exposed the ones like me, who passed among the whites with my blue eyes and light brown hair. Ultimately, my cells betrayed the true nature of my ancestry. I was categorized accordingly. Making a baby with a man who was white was forbidden for me, for him, for us.

I felt first the flutters, then the kicks, then the foot lodged under my ribs, then the hiccups. I talked to the baby. I knew it was a boy, and I named him Diego, for my father. At night, I would look at the sky and tell him the names of all the stars I knew, which wasn't that many. When the Perseids came, I went out on the roof to see them, and while I watched, I sang a lullaby to him, palomita blanca, palomita azul. I sang to him every night.

Exercise was good for the baby, the nurse said, so they allowed me daily walks in my neighborhood. My walk took me down a street where there was a park on one side and an empty lot on the other. One day, I paused by the lot to watch the monarch butterflies on the milkweed that was growing there. The construction planned for this space would bulldoze all of this—the milkweed, the monarchs, everything.

I nodded at a woman walking by, she was a bit older than me, her skin a light brown, a curl escaped from her hat. You are having a baby, she said. It was not a question. I realized for the first time that others could see my growing belly.

Yes, I said. I'm having a boy.

As I stood there, a monarch landed on my shoulder, orange and black, delicate legs and antennae. They have blessed you, the woman whispered.

Who did, I said.

They have blessed you, she whispered again. They have blessed him. She pointed to the sky. I realized she meant the ancestors. It was forbidden to speak of them. More rules.

After that, I started to smile at people I passed on my walk, though they were all strangers to me. I'm having a baby boy, I would say, even though no one asked. I can't wait to meet him, I would say, even though I knew I never would. I would sing the lullaby, llévame en tus alas a ver a Jesús.

One day, I took the bus down Mass Ave. to the man's house to try to see him. I wanted to ask him to change his mind about registering the baby in the system. I planned to tell him that I would raise the baby, and we would not see him again.

After I got off the bus, I walked down the man's street. I stood outside the blue house I was no longer welcome in. I had only ever been there at night when no one would see me. It was even more beautiful than I realized, with tall windows and elegant arches around the front porch. The front yard was a perfectly green lawn. The shrubs were tamed. There was no milkweed, no monarchs. No blessings.

A delivery van pulled up in front. The driver got a large box out of the back and wheeled it toward the house. As I walked up, I saw from the box that it was a crib. He rang the doorbell, and a woman who did not appear to be pregnant opened the door to let him in. She had red hair. This is how I learned the man had married. And was expecting a child.

When my labor started, it triggered the alarm on the bracelet. The ambulance came, two medics and a police officer. They made me walk down the stairs and climb onto the gurney that was waiting in the lobby. My hand was cuffed to the gurney. They took me to Mass General.

I was asleep when the baby was delivered. When I woke, it

was the next day. There was a bandage across my belly where they had taken the baby out. They would have also taken precautions to ensure that this never happened again. I had read that in the packet. There was a blue mark inked on the inside of my left wrist that would not come off when I scrubbed it with soap.

At the hospital, they wouldn't let me see the baby. I wept most of that day and most of that night. They gave me a sedative so that I wouldn't upset the other patient in my shared room. As my thoughts started to flutter, I heard soft weeping from the other side of the curtain. I began to sing the lullaby I had sung to the baby, the one my mother had sung to me when I was a little girl, palomita blanca, palomita azul.

The morning of the third day after my baby was born, it was sunny outside. I got up to dress in the clothes that I had come into the hospital with. I looked up just as the man and his wife walked by the door. Drawn by my motion in the room, the man's wife looked in through the door for a moment. She was carrying a newborn in her arms.

The nurse would not answer my questions about the man or my baby. I wanted to know if he had taken my child. A home has been provided, was all the nurse would say, before she called security to restrain me from running after the man and his wife and my child.

I was given pills to take home with me. They softened the grief, which felt like a ledge. My belly was still swollen, but I was alone in my own body for the first time in months. A few days after the birth, the nurse came to examine me. She said my stomach would return to flatness, my milk would dry up. She did not suggest that I might have another child someday.

A few days later, after listening to the Leader's nightly address, I got back on the bus and went to the man's house. The number on the keypad was the one I still remembered. I opened the back door and crept up the stairs to the small room where I thought the baby might be.

The baby's room was painted blue, wooden block letters on the wall told me that his name was James. This is how I learned I was right: he was a boy. I turned down the baby monitor so we would not be heard.

I leaned over the crib and looked at my son for the first time. He had light brown hair, nearly blond. It might stay that color, I thought, or it might turn brown like mine. I wondered what color his eyes would be. His skin was pale, like mine. But the ancestors knew.

His lips made a soft, suckling motion as I lifted him out of the crib and held him to me. I sat down on the floor, afraid that the rocker would make too much noise. I put my baby to my breast and nursed him. At first, he fed lazily, full of sleep, then more urgently. My body eased, relaxed, relieved, as the milk let down, flowed into him, warm, nourishing.

Diego, I whispered. As I lay him back in his crib, I saw that inside of his wrist had a small, blue mark that matched mine.

For many nights, we did this, always after the man and his wife turned out their lights for the night. Diego was always drowsy during these times, but occasionally he would open his eyes and look at me while he nursed, his hand a small fist that waved without much conviction, sometimes landing on my face, his fingers tiny explorers on my lips and nose.

I sang the lullaby to him in a voice that was softer than soft, si, niñito bueno, yo te llevaré. I brought a tiny blue bird made of ceramic that I would show him. Then I would kiss his small hands as they wrapped around my fingers. He never cried when I was there. He never cried when I put the blue bird back in my pocket and left.

One night, I forgot to turn down the monitor. I looked up and the man's wife was standing in the doorway of the room. She waited silently for us to finish.

There was no thought of making a scene. Goodbye, Diego, I whispered, kissing his forehead for the last time as I handed him back to the man's wife. She took him without a word, but when I reached to retrieve the bird from where I had left it on the side table, she finally spoke. Leave it, she said.

She followed me as I walked down the back stairs and out of the house. Standing on the porch, I turned to her. Her face was opaque, and she said, in a manner that was something like gentle, his name is James. She handed me a piece of paper and then she closed the door.

As I walked away, I looked at what she had handed me—a small photograph of my son. But when I came back the next night, the code on the keypad had been changed. That night, I slept in the backyard. When I woke, my body was aching with cold and my breasts full of milk for Diego. After that, they moved away, and I could not find where.

I returned to my life before I had met the man, before he put the baby in me, before they took him from me. I continued my research job, and when my coworkers asked where I'd been, I told them I'd been sick. I lived in the same small one-bedroom apartment. But I did not forget Diego.

Every night after the Leader's address, I would go out. Sometimes I sat in the park across from the empty lot, and I sang the lullaby, porque con tu mami te has portado bien. One night, I saw the same woman I had spoken with before. Where is your baby, she asked. I could not bring myself to tell her that they had taken him from me, she saw it in my eyes. He was blessed, was all she said. And we sat there a moment and looked out on the lot, which was no longer empty, but half-filled with construction. No milkweed. No monarchs.

V.C. MCCABE

Geometries of Benediction

Hidden, she, of cloven hoof, kicking fire,
devours the fog-cloaked mountaintops, rustles
burnished bronze dreams fallen, broken,
ritual sacrifices offered on Autumn's altar.

Two young bucks lock antlers, fighting for
dominance, while the world refracts like a
crushed prism, kaleidoscopic & lost.

Milk spilt on shattered glass, domestic shards.

Skyscraper remorse desiccated in desert sun,
your certainty trembles in thimble time. In
situ tableau, a morgue of truth, what contempt,
what grace, a form of recompense, a river spent.

Softly, softly, the soil indents over a grave.
Starlings, a grackle, a rattle, a snake. Away,
we explore the geometries of benediction.

Shimmering insects, my kin, burrow beneath
my skin, growing roots in my veins. We trees,
bent, dark, twisted, monstrous—adore us.

Excess of sound, a song, a chorus of skeletons,
bones of my innocence, my sepulchral youth.

Breathing in orbit, the atmospheric wake, empty
of malice, of mercy, I taste
sweet destruction—our holy, our god.

Tuesday May Never Come

The Price is Right is on television in the media room again, and no matter how many times Bernie's seen it, he can't guess the price of a can of Hunt's tomato sauce to save his life, which Laura teases him about every time he gets it wrong, and she guards the remote on her wheelchair's armrest where he can't reach it from the couch, hasn't been able to reach it in the three months since his kids sold his house and abandoned him at Suncoast Senior Living, where Laura is always first to the media room and the remote, and he wants to complain about how unfair it all is to Patty, his wife of fifty-something years, who knew the exact dates of the kids' birthdays, the anniversaries, all the grandkids' names and ages, just like she would have known he doesn't want to watch *The Price is Right* because *Law & Order* reruns are playing on another channel, the original *L & O*, none of those spin-offs which he hates, and Patty would know what day it was, because all Bernie knows is it isn't Tuesday, because if today were Tuesday, Laura would be wheeled off to bingo with her clucking girlfriends, and he'd have the remote on the couch next to him, and he could play detective for a little while, solve cases with Detective Briscoe, the grizzled vet who doesn't have time for anyone slowing him down as he hunts murderers and brings them to justice, and Bernie wonders who Detective Briscoe is partnered with this episode, he's had a few partners over the years, and on Tuesdays that's how it is for Bernie, he's the new partner, and

Det. Briscoe assesses him, wondering if he's up to snuff, if he has what it takes, what horrors he's seen, and Bernie could tell him about his thirty years on the road as a corporate accounts manager for a national coffee chain, and true horror is all the time he spent away from his family, and when he thinks back on the years the images cycle through many things he wishes he could forget, peeking over the curtains during Patty's three C-sections, watching the doctors pull the babies past her intestines, wondering if she'd ever be put back right, or Patty's voice on the phone calls to him on the road, the phone call when their oldest boy cut his wrist in their bathroom, or the phone call the first time their baby girl returned home with a purple bruise on her cheek and claimed she fell, or the phone call about how their middle-child moved out in the middle of the night without saying goodbye, or how after fifty-something years he rose out of bed one morning and Patty didn't, though they agreed when it was time for them to go he should go first, how after all those years of being a husband, a father, he didn't know how to be either, and all those retirement years of watching *Law & Order* reruns he didn't have the first clue what to do when he couldn't wake his dear, sweet Patty, didn't know which of his kids to call or if they would answer, didn't know how to tell them, didn't know how to talk to them, had never really talked to them, and what does he have to say other than he's sorry, it should be him, but before he can tell Det. Briscoe any of that and settle the question of his fitness for duty, they're grabbing their suit coats and rushing out of the precinct, because there's always another body on Tuesday, another case to solve, and he knows to stay close because Det. Briscoe knows exactly what to do, who to call, what comes next, he's a great partner, and Bernie hasn't had a new partner for fifty-plus years, and yes, he could ask Laura to change the channel, could tell her all about Tuesdays and the cases he investigates while she's stamping green ink on numbered squares, how life is unfair, how little people value it and how quickly it can be taken away, how one day will be the last day he watches *Law & Order*, and he'll be under a sheet and his life will remain a mystery he was never able to solve, and Bernie turns to Laura, and her head slowly creaks in his direction, and she's squinting at him, hand on the remote, studying him as if he's a prize on the Showcase Showdown she's never seen before, while he wonders if she's up to snuff, if she has what it takes, what horrors she's seen.

No Context Autoimmune Disorder

The night a bottle of three-dollar hand wash tries to take me out, I solve Letter Boxed in two words for the first time. I remember my answer—"Aviator–Reblochon." It wasn't the official solution (probably because I used 'O' too many times), but it did conjure up an amusing visual of a piloting cheese in shades. Across the A&E, an agitated man under the influence shoves a chair at an orderly, and eight security officers charge in. (Eight?) One has Nyan Cat as his ringtone in the year 2022. I give the doctor too much information she doesn't need, and tell the nurse administering the antihistamine jab I'm weird about needles. She asks if that means I will scream, and I say only if she doesn't swab me properly pre-injection. On the way home, an otter from a nearby park crosses the road; I miss it because my eyes are closed. Surviving sea salt-scented attempted murder is exhausting.

RACHEL FEIRMAN

"Inky Night"
Digital art, 8 x 10 inches, February 2022

Rachel's various outlets of creativity include making digitally illustrated artworks, traditional artwork using acrylic paints, gouache, watercolor, and a method called linocut printing. She most enjoys the method of digital art because of the ease it creates in trying new things, and putting her artwork on a vast selection of surfaces such as photo paper, buttons, stickers, textiles, and more!

Just Like Her but Selling Pharmaceuticals

On set, it's never easy to concentrate.

On set, with all the lights and cameras and make-up and costumes and props and art and fellow talent. *Talent*, the word always makes me snicker. But then through the trailer mirror I spot the actress who is playing my sister, and boom, I'm floored. Not because she is beautiful. (She is.) Not because she is famous. (She isn't.) But because she is a dead ringer for my lover who died three years ago today.

On set, same face, a decade ago, we met. The same long forehead with a concentration vein running down the symmetry of the same nose, almost flat at the eyes, a cutie upturn at the tip. Same chiselled jaw jutting past succulent, strong lips. Can't help but stare, side-eyed, scrolling madly through the inner hard-drive. Her laughter at the hairdresser's crack echoes around a sealed-off-for-safety goldmine.

On set, the first and second scenes flit by in a blur. Must have nailed my lines. What lines? *ProCare provides outstanding customer care and convenient home delivery for the mailing of prescription medications and medical supplies to qualified patients with diabetes and chronic illnesses.* What marks? Tape on the floor. What are marks and lines but emotional milestones and what-stones because the director says nothing but good job, guys. Good job.

At lunch, we sit beside each other. Trade Instagram accounts. I call up an old photo, smiling happy, embracing, post-show, my lover in a flamenco dress, all long haired and tanned and healthy. I hold the phone over her corn and beans and sparkling water and say you know you look exactly like someone I used to love, loved, still love.

On set, does love end at death, I don't ask.

Doesn't she look like you?

Yes, she does, a lot. Who is it?

She's dead. We almost married.

Oh, I am so sorry.

Forgive me if I stare. I'm not a creep.

I do look like her.

You're her resurrection. I can't stop looking. Sorry, if that's freaky.

It is freaky.

I'll try not to stare, and if I act weird, it's that, not you. Just me. Her. You. Sorry.

What happened?

Ovary. Er. Ovarian cancer. Three weeks. Wasn't even fully diagnosed.

Stare away.

On set, I do. All the time wondering how what I said makes her feel and having no idea.

On set, I try to imagine not to imagine. I try to use the past tense. The present tense feels unfaithful. Our future tense has passed away. I try to use my empathy muscles, but they are chess moves just out of mental reach.

On set, I don't know if my lover still feels and is watching and laughing and even put this coincidence, herself, in my path to help me remember.

On set, memories are gorgeous tools, as much as us, this actress, this set house, this set family. We play the story, are paid to deliver. Ready. Sound. Set. Rolling. Action.

On set, we have a scene where we must hug. Not a dramatic moment, just a normal, good-to-see-you, sis. The director, with technical motives, asks for more than eleven takes. Each hug brings us closer and closer to a finished past. A place rarely captured properly on screen. Each hug gets longer and longer until I am holding on to I don't know what.

Each hug sells the pharmaceuticals better and better *home delivery for the mailing of prescription medications and medical supplies to qualified patients with diabetes and chronic illnesses* until the actress playing my sister whispers secretly in my ear, I don't mind, I feel what you're doing, you're doing fine, but let's keep this professional.

ically **DONALD GUADAGNI**

Daydreams

Bic black ink ballpoint pen, 8.5 x 11 inches, May 1998
Part of a once a decade series started in 1980
including pieces "Desolation" and "Teru's song"
(Next Page)

Daydreams is an ideal that represents serene isolation, that which conveys elements not normally found together but are spiritual norms for myself that I find to be complete and embrace places and seasons. The creation of simple pen ink is in my mind the purest form of non verbal communications, the images are emotionally driven and convey the inner currents of unspoken dreams and turmoil that refuse to be defined by mere words. My art remains the truest reflection of how I view the world and how my inner self seeks to share each fleeting glimpse I choose to share.

Old Photos

For Ahmaud Arbery...
...Brionna Taylor, George Floyd, Jordan Davis, Eric Garner, Cynthia Graham Hurd, Rev. DePayne Middleton-Doctor, Rev. Dr. Daniel Simmons, Sr., Ethel Lee Lance, Rev. Sharonda Ann Coleman-Singleton, Susie J. Jackson, Tywanza Sanders, Myra Thompson, Rev. Clementa C. Pinckney, Gynnya McMillen, Walter Scott, Donovan Lewis, Amir Locke, Fanta Bility...

A fresh death no matter what I do.
Chased up, then a cold Georgia shootdown.
There will be no new photos of you.

Men and bullets split our time in two:
Before and after your run in that town.
A fresh death no matter what I do

In good ole Georgia, these cowardly two
called you outta your name; followed you 'round.
There will be no new photos of you.

Again. Again. Stillness governs our view.
One mother now wears a mourner's crown.
A fresh death no matter what I do.

Ceremonies go long; life's now a different hue.
A still smile flashes in skin deep brown.
There will be no new photos of you.

There will be no new photos of you.
Not your voice; not nary a sound.
A fresh death no matter what I do.
There will be no new photos of you.

R E N E E   C R O N L E Y

A chronically unhealthy health care system

from years of gluttony and bloat
and eating itself from the inside
gains weight in all the wrong places

while the organs scream for nutrients
but are starved into submission
and told they have enough to survive

the mouth spouts out grand promises
and spreads them thin over bare bones
of skeleton crews hidden behind policies

until their lip service dries and cracks
and the consequences bleed out
and finally show their teeth.

CONTRIBUTORS

Samuel A. Adeyemi is a writer and editor from Nigeria. A Best of the Net Nominee and Pushcart Nominee, he is the winner of the *Nigerian Students Poetry Prize* 2021. His manuscript was selected by Kwame Dawes and Chris Abani for the *New-Generation African Poets* chapbook box set, 2022. His works have appeared in *Palette Poetry, Frontier Poetry, 580 Split, Strange Horizons, Agbowo, Isele Magazine, Brittle Paper, Jalada*, and elsewhere.

Mario Aliberto III is a Pushcart nominated writer whose work is forthcoming or published with *The Sonora Review, Rejection Letters, Tahoma Literary Review* and others. He lives in Tampa Bay with his wife and daughters, and yet the dog still runs the house. Twitter: @marioaliberto3.

Esperanza Cintrón is the author of *Shades, Detroit Love Stories*, a 2020 Michigan Notable Book, published by Wayne State University Press. Her short story "Shadow Dancer" was nominated for a Pushcart Prize. She has three books of poetry: *Visions of a Post-Apocalyptic Sunrise*, the Naomi Long Madgett Award winner *What Keeps Me Sane*, and *Chocolate City Latina*. Cintrón's work appears in *Manteca! An Anthology of Afro-Latin@ Poets*; *Mamas, Martyrs, and Jezebels*; *Obsidian* and others. She was a Callaloo Writing Fellow at Brown and Oxford Universities, the recipient of a Michigan Council for the Arts Individual Artist Grant, a National Endowment for the Humanities educator's scholarship and has a doctorate in English literature from the State University of New York at Albany. Under the *nom de plume* Alegra Verde, she has written several short works of fiction many of which have been translated into various languages.

Renee Cronley is a writer and nurse from Manitoba. She studied Psychology and English at Brandon University, and Nursing at Assiniboine Community College. Her work appears or is forthcoming in *Chestnut Review, PRISM international, Off Topic, Love Letters to Poe, NewMyths. com, Weird Little Worlds, ParABnormal Magazine, Black Spot Books*, and several other anthologies and literary magazines.

Steve Denehan lives in Kildare, Ireland with his wife Eimear and daughter Robin. He is the author of two chapbooks and three poetry collections. Winner of the Anthony Cronin Poetry Award and twice winner of Irish Times' New Irish Writing, his numerous publication credits include *Poetry Ireland Review* and *Westerly*.

Rachel Feirman is a traditional and digital artist living in Ithaca, NY, who seeks inspiration from the beauty and vibrancy found in her natural surroundings. Rachel's motivation for her art is to make a connection with you, the viewer! She offers art created with her own vision and life experiences, and hopes her twist on the many aspects of nature helps to bring a newfound perspective to your life. She creates digitally illustrated artworks using Procreate on the Ipad with the Apple Pencil, and traditional artwork using acrylic paints, gouache, watercolor, and a method called linocut printing. Twitter: @rachelradishart.

Donald Guadagni is an international educator, author, and writer currently teaching and conducting research in Beijing China. His published work includes fiction, non-fiction, poetry, prose, science fiction, fantasy, humor, academic, romance, humor, and true crime. International photography and his artwork. Former iterations include military, law enforcement, prisons, engineering, and forever the wayward son.

Natalie Harris-Spencer is an English writer, digital editor, and blogger living in America. Her work has appeared in *Subnivean, Stonecoast Review, Hobart, The Dark City, The Satirist*, and others. She is the winner of the *Chestnut Review* Stubborn Writers Contest, the Hummingbird Flash Fiction Prize, and she was selected by *Oyster River Pages* as one of their Emerging Fiction Voices. She earned her MFA in Creative Writing at Stonecoast, and she is the Editor-in-Chief of Aspiring Author. She is currently working on her debut novel. Natalie enjoys surprise in fiction. And tea. Twitter: @NRHarrisSpencer, IG: @natalie.harris.spencer.

Judy Kaber is the current Poet Laureate of Belfast, Maine. Her poems have been published in journals such as *Atlanta Review, december, and Spillway*. Contest credits include the *Maine Postmark Poetry* Contest in 2009, second place in the 2016 *Muriel Craft Bailey Contest*, and the *Maine Poets Society Contest*, 2021. Her poems also appear in the following anthologies: *Enough: Poems of Resistance and Protest, Wait: Poems from the Pandemic, and Balancing Act2: An Anthology of Poems by Fifty Maine Women*. She has three chapbooks: Renaming the Seasons, In Sleep We Are All the Same and A Pandemic Alphabet.

Katie Kemple's work can also be found online in the following journals: *Rattle, Rust + Moth, SOFTBLOW, Valparaiso Poetry Review*, and *Whale Road Review*.

Sharon Lin is a poet and essayist. Her work appears in *The New York Review of Books, WIRED, Diode, Sine Theta*, and elsewhere and is anthologized in *Best New Poets 2021* and *Voices of the East Coast* (Penmanship Books). She lives in New York City.

Alison Lubar teaches high school English by day and yoga by night. They are a queer, nonbinary, mixed-race femme whose life work (aside from wordsmithing) has evolved into bringing mindfulness practices, and sometimes even poetry, to young people. Their work has been nominated for both the Pushcart & Best of the Net, and they're the author four chapbooks: *Philosophers Know Nothing About Love* (Thirty West Publishing House, 2022), *queer feast* (Bottlecap Press, 2022), *sweet euphemism* (CLASH!, Spring 2023), and *it skips a generation* (Stanchion, Fall 2023). You can find out more at http://www.alisonlubar.com or on Twitter @theoriginalison.

Jennifer Luh is a writer and lawyer based in the San Francisco Bay Area. She studied neuroscience at UCLA and is a graduate of Harvard Law. This is her first fiction publication. Instagram: @jennifer.luh | Twitter: @LuhJennifer.

V.C. McCabe is the author of the forthcoming collection *Ophelia* (Femme Salvé Books, 2023) and *Give the Bard a Tetanus Shot* (Vegetarian Alcoholic Press, 2019). She was a music journalist for Pulitzer Prize-winning newspaper *The Charleston Gazette* and edited for *Frontier Poetry, Ice Floe Press, and Barren Magazine*. Her work appears in ekphrastic exhibits and journals worldwide, including *EPOCH, Poet Lore, and Prairie Schooner.* An Appalachian poet, she has lived in Ireland, England, and West Virginia. Her website is vcmccabe.com.

Michael Moreth is a recovering Chicagoan living in the micropolitan City of Sterling, the Paris of Northwest Illinois.

Yvette R. Murray is an award-winning poet and writer. She has been published in *Emrys Journal, A Gathering Together, litmosphere*, forthcoming in *Chestnut Review* and elsewhere. She is the 2022 Susan Laughter Meyers Poetry Fellow, a 2022 Watering Hole Fellow, a 2021 Best New Poet selection, and a Pushcart Prize nominee. Find her on Twitter @MissYvettewrites.

DM O'Connor has an MFA from University College Dublin & the University of New Mexico. He is a contributing reviewer for *Rhino Poetry* and fiction editor at *Bending Genres*. His work has appeared in *Splonk*, *A New Ulster*, *Fractured Lit*, *Cormorant*, *Crannog*, *Opossum*, *CRAFT*, *The New Quarterly*, *The Irish Times*, *The Guardian*, and others. In 2021 he was the recipient of the Cuirt International Award for Fiction, the Tom Gallon Short Story Award, and a writer-in-residence at the Kerouac House. He is grateful for the support of the Arts Council of Ireland and Words Ireland.

Mollie O'Leary is a poet from Massachusetts. She holds an MFA in poetry from the University of Washington. Mollie's chapbook *The Forgetting Curve* is forthcoming through Poetry Online's offline.onl chapbook series. Her work has appeared in *Frontier Poetry*, *Poetry Online*, *DIALOGIST*, and elsewhere. Mollie has participated in workshops through Tin House and Inprint, and also attended residencies in Mexico, Italy, and Norway. She reads for *GASHER Journal*.

Max Pasakorn (he/she/they) is a queer, Thai-born, Singapore-based writer, poet, and spoken word artist. They are one of the founding members of the Singapore-based writing collective /stop@BadEndRhymes (/s@ber). Read more about Max at www.maxpasakorn.works and follow Max on Instagram at @maxpsk_writes.

Sofia T. Romero is a writer and editor who lives in the Boston area. Her work has appeared in several publications, including *Necessary Fiction*, *Rigorous*, and *Waterwheel Review*. She is the author of the forthcoming story collection, *We Have Always Been Who We Are*. Her website is sofiatromero.com.

Allison Thung is a poet and project manager from Singapore. Her poetry has been published in *ANMLY, Emerge Literary Journal, Lumiere Review, Roi Fainéant Press*, and elsewhere. Find her on Twitter @poetrybyallison or at www.allisonthung.com.

Julian Wong was born in Boston and raised in Hong Kong. As a youth in Hong Kong, Wong studied traditional Chinese painting with renowned artist Chao Shao An. He has Bachelors of Arts in Painting from the University of California at Santa Cruz and in Industrial Design from California College of Arts, San Francisco. His work appears in collections around the world and in various publications. An accomplished industrial designer, Wong is a member of the Hatch Art Studio and has worked with DDOT, Crate & Barrel and others.

Colin Xu is a photographer based in Philadelphia, PA. His work has been published in *Pennsylvania Magazine*, *Down East Magazine*, and in local galleries.

Chestnut Review
VOLUME 4 NUMBER 4 SPRING 2023
FOR STUBBORN ARTISTS

COVER ART

Grace Zhou
"Inhibition"
Digital artwork, 16x10 inches. September 24, 2022

Chestnut Review

VOLUME 4 NUMBER 4 SPRING 2023

Chestnut Review LLC, Ithaca, New York
chestnutreview.com

Chestnut Review appears four times a year online, in January, April, July, and October, and once per year in print in July.

ISSN 2688-0350 (online), ISSN 2688-0342 (print)

CONTENTS

Introduction

Spring is a time of blossoming. A viewing of cherry trees in bloom is called hanami, 花見. We welcome you under our branches to read our Spring offerings, bud by bud, petal by petal. This issue rounds out our fourth year and concludes Volume 4. Our editorial team and staff look forward to unfurling new branches in the upcoming months.

We are celebrating an incipient new chapbook, Dacia Price's *This is for the Naming*, which was the winner of the 2022 Prose Chapbook Contest. This will be on our site in May, and in the meantime we invite you to read the interview and excerpt as a promise of what will be in the full version, which will be released in mid-May.

At AWP in Seattle we met in joy, conviviality, and excitement for the year ahead. We recently had our first retreat in Mexico and are anticipating our second in Wales in June. We have taken our chapbook contests and turned them into a press model of publication that will be open each spring and fall. We hope to nurture these initiatives and others into offshoots, opportunities for our community. We are grateful for the feedback we receive from you, our readers, submitters, and contributors, about how our mission and vision for Chestnut Review is reaching you, the roots and resilience of our trunk.

DACIA PRICE

2022 PROSE CHAPBOOK CONTEST WINNER

Mitosis

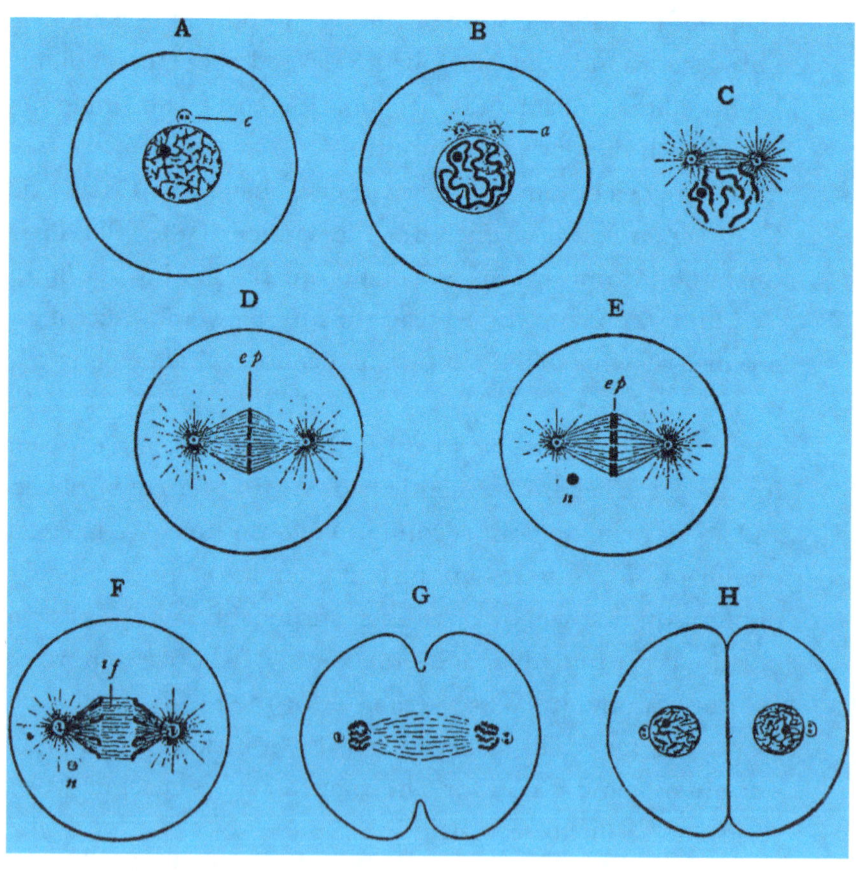

Intraphase: *Homeostasis; the phase before. Each chromosome makes an exact copy of itself so that the cell has two identical sets.*

I inherited my mother's skin: quick to burn, temperamental, prone to acne blooms. At forty-five my mother needed two different skin creams: one to treat deepening lines and wrinkles and the other to quiet the acne that continued, undaunted, in the creases between her nose and cheek, in the deep crevice of her chin. Her skin was a tapestry of scars both healed and emerging: pinched and knotted, then swollen red. In summer she wore wide brimmed hats and thick sunblock that left her reflective and two shades lighter. Later, she'd blame this too for breakouts.

Until I turned twenty, I believed I had escaped this inheritance. My skin was clear and then it wasn't. Inside my body was a gene waiting to be turned on.

Prophase: *The nuclear membrane disintegrates, the nucleolus disappears, and the centrosomes move toward opposite poles of the cell.*

There is an aroma to thunderstorms that is both sweet and pungent. This is the smell of ozone, created when lightning splits atmospheric nitrogen and oxygen molecules to form nitric oxide. Ozone is carried in the air ahead of the rain giving storms their distinctive smell. Despite its association with the Great American Plains, Tornado Alley reaches as far north as southern Ontario where the warm air from the Great Lakes collides with the cool air from the north. Every year Ontario sees twenty-five to thirty tornados, though it's common for this area to see more. Before a tornado develops, ozone combines with sudden, heavy humidity. Everything falls silent. The aroma is warning and stagnant earth. From the living room window we watch as clouds gather in the distance, the light is tinged green and the hair on our bodies becomes charged with electricity.

In 1985 an EF4 struck a neighborhood in Barrie, Ontario where my aunt and uncle lived with their three children. The rain that had been falling all afternoon obscured the body of the half mile wide tornado so completely that no one saw it coming. At 5pm my aunt put the baby to bed upstairs and when she came back down, the living room window blew in. She had just enough time to barricade herself and her two older children in the basement before the house was overtaken. The sound of shattering glass and buckling wood—indistinguishable from the roar of the wind.

Photos from that day show a staircase and a second floor bedroom standing in a sea of debris. There are no images of my aunt or cousins, no pictures of the neighbors who braved the exposed stairs to uncover the baby left sleeping in her crib, nothing to document the miracle of her still alive shape, reunited in the arms of her mother.

When I ask my aunt why she thinks my cousin survived, she credits an extra thick quilt, tucked between the crib rails.

Prometaphase: *The nuclear envelope around the chromosomes breaks down. Now there is no nucleus and the sister chromatids are free.*

Accutane is a vitamin A derived medication used to treat severe acne. It works by altering the body's DNA transcription to decrease the size and output of sebaceous glands while also making those glands less sticky so that acne is harder to form. Like vitamin A, Accutane accumulates in body tissue so should be taken under strict observation by a doctor and never for longer than 20 weeks.

Side effects include but are not limited to || skin sensitivity || dry skin || chapped lips || itchy skin || thinning hair || excessive skin peeling || increased acne || muscle aches and pains || headaches || psychosis || suicide ideation || cornea ulcers || night blindness || an increase in liver enzymes causing jaundice and hepatitis || profound birth defects || congenital heart disease || missing eyes || hydrocephalus || microcephaly. Patients taking Accutane must have long term birth control measures in place as well as a backup method for pregnancy prevention like condoms or spermicides. If pregnancy occurs, termination is recommended.

I was thirteen when my mother finished her first cycle of Accutane and seventeen when she finished her second. Neither round cured her acne.

Metaphase: *The spindle fibers attach and line up the chromosomes along the center of the cell.*

I find a mouse at the bottom of an empty bin of dog food. It must have fallen in and as its tiny paws slipped against the slick plastic walls, realized it couldn't get itself back out. It is a defeated ball of gray curled in the scoop. At first, I believe I have found a dead mouse in the dog food but as I lift the bin the mouse jumps, and I then jump, and then both of us nearly fall on the floor. I have only seen mice in pet store cages; running in plastic wheels and burrowed deep behind glass panels or metal bars. I have no idea what to do with something so wild, set loose inside my home. I take the bin to the backyard and gently tilt it until the mouse slides across and then over the bin's lip, touching the ground and disappearing beneath a rock. I am not so close to the house but not so far away either.

Later, I hear scratching in the walls and attic; I count tiny mouse footprints by the back door; I notice miniscule tunnels beneath layers of snow. At night I hear burrowing above my head and I am plagued by thoughts of mice chewing through ceiling tiles; growing enormous on a diet of insulation and dust. In my restless half-sleep mice become rats, become squirrels, become undefined mutations of *rodent*, their edges indistinguishable from the dark corners in which they hide. I am paralyzed by the unknowing.

Anaphase: *The spindle fibers pull the sister chromatids away from each other, toward opposite ends of the cell. This step is essential, ensuring that each daughter cell will have a complete set of chromosomes.*

In the basement my aunt's arms are wrapped around two of her children while she prays for her third to be spared. She bargains and negotiates. She tells me how close she came to running upstairs and into the storm, how it was the grip of those older two that persuaded her to stay. They would follow, she tells me, and then she'd be responsible for the deaths of them all.

My infant cousin grows into a woman who is deaf in her right ear, who cannot have children, who adopts animals instead. Currently, she has four dogs and a single gray cat. She makes a living baking dog-friendly doughnuts out of peanut butter and oat flour and pumpkin puree which she sells online.

My aunt believes my cousin's deafness and sterility are transactional, the price paid for life. When the doctors find a mass in my aunt's breast she feels relief. Finally, she tells me, she'll get the chance to repay the debt herself.

Telophase: *The mitotic spindle breaks down and a nuclear membrane begins to form around each set of daughter chromosomes.*

Cancer is domestic, a mutation of the body without a means for self correction. Left alone, the body consumes itself: cell replication amped up; gone haywire; out of control, until a mutated cell infiltrates liver then kidney and lungs; depositing itself in the body's blood to be carried to organ after organ until each is littered with displaced bits of something else. Tiny colon cells living inside organs that are not colon.

The images taken of my mother's insides are splatter art. Dark spots in her lower left lung, both kidneys, her liver, stomach. There's little we can do, the doctor tells us. How could she not have known, I want to know, how could they have missed this? Such small things are hard to see, he says, and your mother, she had no symptoms.

Maybe it was the meat, my mother says, I always ate too much red meat. Or the dairy. Maybe, she says, it was that second round of Accutane. She imagines molecules of vitamin A lingering in tissue that was once colon. She wants to know if they can cause cancer. She wants to know what she did wrong. She is desperate to find a thing to blame.

Cytokinesis: *The cell membrane pinches in at the cell equator, forming a cleft called the cleavage furrow. This is the final splitting of mother cell into identical daughter cells.*

I linger in corners sniffing out the aroma of dead mouse. *Putrescence*—the inceptive form of *putrid*—is the name given to the scent of decaying flesh, but I smell only dust and paint and the staleness of air too long enclosed.

The man who comes to eradicate the mice was once a doctor and I feel strangely reassured, as though this caring for humans might transfer to the mice living in the spaces between house and not house. The poison he uses targets only them, he says, and I have translated poison to mean medicine to assuage my guilt. They'll seek the outside and die somewhere else, he tells me, but I'm not so sure. I want to believe but wanting and doing are not the same thing. When he leaves I type: *How long does it take for a mouse to decompose?* into the search engine of my phone while my nose is pressed into the corner where wall meets wall, furiously inhaling. *Two weeks in warm weather*, I read. Outside the snow continues to fall. *Much longer in the cold.* I read about how coffee grounds and charcoal can mask the scent of dead rodent. *Orange peels*, the text says, *are another aromatic choice.*

I read about the way disease alters a person's aroma. Untreated diabetics—for example—can smell like nail polish. Cancer doesn't have a defined aroma. Still, there are electronic noses in development to sniff it out; technology based on the olfactory glands of dogs. Dogs can detect cancer in urine samples with 98% accuracy. Tests to detect colon cancer are only 79% accurate. My mother took three, each with a negative result. For her, the accuracy of these tests was zero.

I think about the mice that will soon be decomposing in my walls and consider calling the doctor back to remove the boxes of poison he's placed in the attic and basement and underneath the snow piled on the deck but I'm certain it's already been consumed, that death is an act in progress.

A Conversation with Dacia Price, Prose Chapbook Winner

NB: This conversation has been truncated and is available in full on our website; tune in for discussion of the benefit of an MFA, Dacia's research and writing interests, future projects, and thoughts on writing authentic, vulnerable CNF.

MP: Hello everyone! I'm Maria S. Picone, the Managing Editor of Chestnut Review and the Prose Chapbook Editor, and I'm here with a very special guest, which is the 2022 winner of our Prose Chapbook Contest, Dacia Price. Dacia's chapbook, *This is for the Naming*, will be available in mid-May and we're so, so excited to publish her work. Dacia, it's really great to have you here today and illuminate this awesome work that's coming out in the world soon.

DP: Thank you so much for having me! I am so thrilled to have it out in the world and so excited to be here with you.

MP: This chapbook, to me, when I first encountered it, seemed like such a perfectly wedded hybrid of poetical forms and devices and lyricism with these small, CNF flash that are strung together or braided. How did the genesis of the project come to be? Have you been somebody who's always worked in this hybrid form or was this something you developed?

DP: I think I've always aspired to work in hybrid form and the deeper I get into my craft and my practice, the more hybrid it becomes, sometimes unintentionally so. I might start out with something that is very straightforward CNF memoir-esque and then through the writing I find myself making more organic, hybrid choices. So I think organically I am a much more hybrid writer than even I anticipate for myself. But this collection actually came about as a result of a challenge of creating a flash piece of CNF every single week underneath a constraint, and the constraint for me was "the things that lurk in the shadows." That was self-imposed, and I found myself writing all these sort of flash pieces that ended up being in conversation with the loss of my mother and cancer, and before I knew it I had created this sort of braided collection that was in conversation with itself.

MP: "Things that lurk in the shadows??" That's so evocative and I can't believe it took you to this place. So, how did you determine—there's a couple devices that are used throughout such as one-paragraph sections with breaks, slashes that are straight, the bar ones, a use of dashes. How did you determine this punctuation and paragraph—stanzagraph—based formal language in which to have this medium?

DP: That's such a good question and I don't know if I have a specific answer on the methodology. Often, it falls down on instinct. For me, when I was putting it together, I kept imagining two voices, a duality within the self, so that there is a call and response, or a thought and a list. So the double lines that you see throughout this piece is an articulation of that two-voice element that I'm trying to navigate in my brain as I'm composing this. Same with the slashes—sometimes I'm using them as a visual representation, sometimes it's breathwork, where I'm wanting my reader to take a big inhale or pause in their breath before they move on. It's visual as well as bodily moments of pause or delineation.

MP: I'm taking notes over here! Another thing that struck me about this collection was your use of italics for dialogue or sometimes just straight—there's no quotation marks; it's not the usual convention of prose; it's more of a poetic or experimental prose convention. Did that also get developed along with this project, where that felt natural?

DP: That one actually felt very intentional. As a reader, I find the typical dialogue markers to be a little boring, a little dull. Some of the writers I admire the most embed their dialogue within the prose itself. It allows the reader to speed through it all so there's not really a difference because there often isn't much of one— the dialogue you're saying, hearing, experiencing is happening in tandem with your experience of that. I love the idea of embedding it and allowing my reader to differentiate between what's being said and what's being experienced.

MP: Wow, I love that! I think it really works, not only with the fact that readers have to do some of that work, but in this idea that it's a two-voice collection talking about the self. It feels more external, like a rupturing, to use these dialogue tags and things. That really kept me reading this collection over and over again in the queue.

A few of your pieces are in hermit crab form, but all of them have an image or, almost a visual aid at the beginning, that introduces a mood, a theme. I love that because, from the title, you can either continue vibing off of that or introduce a different moment or feeling to the collection. When did this gain a visual art component?

DP: I don't know if there was a moment. Each piece went through its own process from construction of lines and narrative and shifted into a visual representation. I'm a very visual person in the way that I interact with the world; I tend to experience things from that place of visual stimulus and so those are often my access points into narrative. I start from a place of scene, of noticing, and then get into the crux of it. Because it starts from this visual origin and goes into narrative, it's a natural progression that it has that visual effect on the page, that we end from a place of visibility.

MP: We talk about voice, and it's almost a cliché, but this collection had such a strong voice. I could feel the author saying, this is the work, this is what I want from it, this is what's here, and, welcome. It felt like one of those magazine spreads with a beautifully curated home and perfect interior decoration—every aspect complemented each other aspect and that made it this rollercoaster ride to read. I was so excited when I saw this for the first time, and I thought to myself, even if she never wants to do a single edit, let's publish it! Of course, it went through a whole reading process, but the first time I read it I was sitting on my couch and my eyes kept getting bigger as I kept scrolling through every page.

DP: That makes my heart swell.

The Song of the Hope Seeker
(*This is for the Naming* Cover Art)

SYDNEY KIM

Your Neighbor Your Lover

At first you wanted him because he had the wide eyes of a housecat, and you could often hear him lifting pots of water onto the stove or the silver noise of him sorting forks and knives into his kitchen drawer through your shared wall. Later you wanted him because when it rained he left his shoes in the hallway, each stuffed with a neat bundle of that Sunday's classifieds, and it was a liquid spring. You remember it raining the entire length of your courtship, the tiny globules of drizzle clinging to the wool of his coat collar, the sudden downpours, the occasional, startlingly profound sunshower. But then his socks started turning up in your laundry and once on your way into the building you dropped a bag of oranges in front of him, and the sight of him chasing an orange into the street was so undignified that you looked up at the telephone wires strung across the very gloomy sky and when you looked back down again he had been clipped by a postal worker on a bicycle and was lying on the ground, insisting you take him to the hospital.

He proposed to you in an upscale restaurant on the Upper East Side, pretended to drop a fork and everything for an excuse to get down on one knee beside the table. He was wearing a suit and you an evening dress, and the whole thing had felt romantic until he was looking up at you with the ring in a small silk box. The restaurant was humid and the floor was slick by the door, the coat closet dripping with long plastic coats, the rain outside a flat and incessant drone beneath the din of voices and steak knives and laughter. There was a famous actor sitting in a booth in the corner who looked up along with the rest of the restaurant when he asked you to marry him. An excited hush fell; the bottles of liquor behind the bar glowed in the half-light, the candle on your table extinguished itself with a wet hiss, and a waiter emerging from the kitchen stopped in his tracks, causing the swinging double doors to knock the tray from his hand so that several entrées and their plates fell to the floor.

No, you said, and you meant it, though it came out more forcefully than you would have liked. He got back into his chair and you both ate the rest of your meal as though nothing had happened. On the way out of the restaurant he insisted on asking for a photo with the famous actor; the actor, who was just putting his fork to a slice of tiramisu, acquiesced, though it was evident that he would have asked to be left alone had he not witnessed, just thirty minutes earlier, the spectacle of the turned-down proposal and been moved by a sliver of pity. You took the picture on your phone and seconds before the flash went off the actor said, rather insincerely, *You two make a lovely couple*, which meant that the reaction this statement evoked was captured, for all eternity, beneath the close-lipped fraud of your lover's photographed smile.

There was nothing wrong with him, necessarily—he had very straight teeth and a full head of hair; he had a basic understanding of hygiene, and was the rare sort of cologne-wearing man who actually wore the correct amount; he did not have any particularly out-of-pocket beliefs about healthcare or climate change; he was one of the rare white men you had been with who had nothing to say about the color of your labia or the potential future attractiveness of your mixed-race children. He was not the sort of man to get worked up about needless things, such as the

length of your pubic hair or how your last ex-boyfriend was still
mailing your things back to you, one by one, with priority ship-
ping. He did, however, have an unfortunate habit of insisting that
he knew you better than you knew yourself, particularly when
it came to sex, and, yes, you knew that this should have been
enough for you to end things, but you were sick of the rain and
enamored with the promise of dry shoes in the morning, and
thus you allowed this to go on, this recurring argument that usu-
ally took place in real-time, during foreplay, his fingers beckoning
knuckle-deep inside of you. That literally doesn't feel good, you
would say, feeling irritated and looking over his shoulder at the
painting of a sunny Machu Picchu on his wall. Or sometimes
the argument would take place more theoretically, while walking
down the street in a light drizzle, or stopping at the mailboxes
in the lobby of your building, and you would feel angry enough
to end things—at least, until he'd slip a bundle of that Sunday's
comics into your shoes before going to bed or open an umbrella
over your head when it was raining so hard the street looked
flooded in silver coins, easy gestures which you mistook for ges-
tures of love, even while you were citing your own body while he
posited the bodies of his ex-girlfriends.

He once told you the problem with you was that good days
made you suspicious. It was one of the truer things he'd ever
said. For example, you had been having a good day prior to the
oranges and the postal worker on the bicycle, and you had felt
suspicious of its lastingness. On the train to the hospital, there
was a woman selling pink umbrella hats. He had his shoulder in
a makeshift sling. He could tell you were annoyed, and this made
him annoyed; he bought an umbrella hat for two dollars and
fifty cents and put it on his head. He said loudly, Are you hav-
ing fun now? You felt embarrassed for everybody in the subway
car and when his name was called in the emergency room you

told him you were going to get some coffee and a slice of lemon cake from the café in the lobby but then took the subway home instead. Outside your apartment building there were still oranges in the street, bright against pavement darkened by that day's rain, which was lukewarm and erratic, soft drizzly spells chased away by a violent torrent which nearly washed the neighbor's Chihuahua into the gutter as it was lifting its leg against the nearest fire hydrant.

The restaurant proposal would not be the only one he would spring upon you over the course of your time together, which, in the scheme of things, was relatively brief and, in retrospect, would have been much more pleasant had it not been continually marred by these sudden and often very public declarations of love. There was the time in Central Park at midday, his pants' knee muddy afterwards and two shirtless men nearby halting their slinging of a frisbee back and forth long enough to watch you shake your head. There was the time on the Brooklyn Bridge amidst the most optimistic of sunshowers, when he knelt in the cyclist lane as if he had learned nothing from the incident with the oranges, and a nearby group of tourists, completely misunderstanding the situation, smiled and clapped from beneath their bubble umbrellas when he stood up and closed the silk box with the ring still inside. It got to the point where you began to chew your food more carefully for fear of cracking a molar on the ring and eventually you went to see a psychiatrist in Morningside Heights to find out why you could not stop turning down his proposals, or, at the very least, why a part of you remained convinced that someday you might surprise yourself by saying yes. The psychiatrist was an alarmingly young white man wearing a yellow button-down shirt and checkered socks whose office was above an eyebrow threading salon. He showed you a series of Rorschachs. You'd thought this was an outdated practice, akin

to astrology or lobotomy, but he appeared to be dead serious
and so you looked at the cards as he held them up. He asked you
what you saw and you wanted to tell him that each and every
one looked like genitalia, except for one which looked like a
monstrous bull with red nostrils, but you had a feeling this might
skew the diagnosis in a less than favorable direction. Ultimately
the fire alarm in the building went off and seeing this psychiatrist
standing on the sidewalk having a conversation, or quite possibly
a dick-swinging contest, with a fireman climbing down from his
loud red truck sufficiently shattered the illusion that he would be
able to tell you anything about yourself that you did not already
know, and so you left without paying for the half-session and
used some of the money to get the peach fuzz threaded from
your upper lip.

Maybe, you thought, if you had never dropped that bag, if
you had never had to see him chase that orange into the street
like that, things might have been different. And sometimes you
even daydreamed what life would be like if you were to knock
down the shared wall between your apartments to make a
home fit for two. But when you mentioned this casually to your
landlord by the mailboxes one morning when you were feel-
ing particularly worn down by the onus of turning down all of
these perfectly earnest proposals, she looked rather alarmed and
told you, in no uncertain terms, that that wall was load-bearing.
What happened in the end was that you were together at another
couple's engagement party when he slipped the ring into your
shot glass while you were salting the back of your hand and, al-
ready drunk, you took it right down with the salt and the tequila
and the lime, your face pinching in the liquor's aftermath before
he even had the chance to get down on one knee, and after the
ensuing endoscopy he told you that he had been thinking and
perhaps he had gotten a little carried away by things and would

need some space to sort things out. You agreed, but neither of your leases were up until the fall and so sometimes, after the rain had lifted and left a strange, sunny city-quiet behind, you could still hear him through the shared wall between your apartments, moving on from you.

"Eden"
(Next Page)
Acrylic, 28x29 inches. November-December 2022

I work in acrylics because of their easy fluidity and cleanup. I also love the brightness of the colors and especially like creating other worldly plants and scenes.

<u>MIMI YANG</u>

Dinner Sonnet

At the cookout past dusk the man who beat his daughter
within an inch of her life is serving the World's Best
Crayfish in a Bucket. We drain butter & brine
from the carapace, think of delicious creatures sweetened
by the belt. the rumen braised by a mother who won't speak
to her son, the silk snapper's mouth gaping with boyish
guilt. Our father, soaking squid in shacha before turning
its body on the spit, selling stories of barbecues in America.
He always leaves out the best part: the night before, his knuckles
browning old bruises, practice for the veal he would tenderize
the next day. Here in the chorus of cicadas, we break bread
in place of daughters, search for God in the backhand
that feeds us. Every dish on the table: an apology he failed
to control. Here. Eat. Savor this death I've spared you.

CAITLYN ALARIO

Lent

chapel smelled like body odor
bible paper & the faint tang
of communion wine, which wasn't wine

but white grape juice in tiny plastic cups.
the youth pastor preached sacrifice & forgiveness
but forgiveness wouldn't come until the end.

for lent, he told us to remember. to think
of jesus in gethsemane, so afraid & forsaken
he's sweating blood, a jesus

who knew what was coming for him.
i knew then i didn't know
what it meant to suffer.

when i thought of gethsemane or golgotha
or god, all i felt was small & uninhabitable.
so much sunday school & i still didn't know

how to pray. i found it impossible
to keep my eyes closed when, years later,
we found a lump in my throat

& every pastor i'd ever known prayed over me.
instead i'd watch the fleshy movements
of their mouths, their hands clasped tightly together.

that's when i learned the violence of surrender.
i wondered if god needed my forgiveness
for giving me more than i could bear.

i learned to pray the same way i learned to suffer.
one day, there was nothing left to do.

Thorns

I slink into the garden at midnight when the moon is high. My footsteps leave pendants of dew in the grass. Around the trunk of Grandpa's lemon tree, I use my hands, then my arms. Embracing at first, then choking. How to asphyxiate the living thing? Twigs concede at my strength; the sound of shorn leaves, a ripple in my ears.

1. In my youth, I'm new as the tree I lie under. I glance up, and my grandmother falters from the portico into the garden with a strange expression on her face. Her knees make a brusque landing; her stretched palms mow the trimmed grass. Stalking after her is my grandfather, sturdy walking oak, under whose bower our many existences have bounded. Now, his hand rises.

The citrus leaves crumple soundlessly, and there's no pleasure in that. So, I begin taking full branches in my hand. One by one, I tear *from* limb *with* limb. Teardrop fruit collapses onto the grassy bed with soft thuds. I snarl with satisfaction; I howl with pride. In the big house behind my shoulders, someone turns on the lights.

2. At dinner, Dad can't sit still. Liquor turns his cheeks ripe, like a triumphant harvest. He rumbles to his feet and kicks the

chair he's sitting on. *Crash*, the joint splinters. At the sight, my mother doesn't stir physically or emotionally—not anymore. She is nuanced in distress, cold to such sprouts of theatricality. Her resilience perturbs my father, who scowling and bedraggled, transfigures into a wooden obstinance. Sonorous and menacing, protected within the bark of his self-image. During our lunar stroll, walking hand in hand, he wolf-growls into my young ears. "The thing about your Mum…" he attempts, reeking frail desperation.

Footsteps approach in the near distance; caution is the chorus of their voices. Under the brunt of my forcible hands, dripping red, the innocent tree quivers. Slowly, we are losing our countenance.

3. The bloodwork says my grandfather and father and I are nearly identical. In the mirror, my lips draw that familiar grimace. Genetic crow's feet perch under my eyes if I smile. My belly is a slow-gestating burl, if I ever stop running or continue drinking, like they did. If my father places his fingers on mine, we are foliage entwined. Decay festers on his skin, and what lies beneath? "The disposition is ingrained," I tell my therapist. "No," she replies. "It isn't."

I'm the terror in the garden, and the new owners' screech sets my periphery ablaze. Arms attempt to deter me, but I lunge ahead, wrap myself definitively around the gaunt tree neck. With a sharp tug, I intend to dissect family history from its physical confine. All history ever needed, anyway, was a large and charged uprooting.

4. As an adult I marry to my liking and start a family, but spend nights haunted by my villains, exonerated without trial.

In the lush afternoon, my husband squeezes the past into icy margaritas and pulls me into his embrace. "You're different," he urges, but I become adamant to uncover the gnarled twist in the path, where Eden turned to rot. "I'm going back there," I insist, but my partner refuses to join. Sloughing off precedence, he takes the kid and leaves, slamming the door inexorably shut.

When the lemon tree budges from its foundation, I creep into a smile. All this time, the residents cloud my ears with warnings. "The police are on their way," or "This isn't your grandfather's house anymore." In my actions, they discern only the pit of every individual's anger: a human outburst. They cannot comprehend as neatly the quiet crimes of the men of my family.

A siren flashes overhead at last, and my pupils glisten wide.

A fresh start reaped with violence, or the bitter consequent sap, can't revoke my past in any measure. Felled by cognition—only a seed, tossed in the epic sunburst—I drop to both knees. The blood that streaks my face is mine alone to tend, and therein lies the wreath of regret, the final reaping—a very good comeuppance.

Spring 2021

I hear the shout before the shot.
K slings a dead diamondback on the wire fence
like hanging clothes on a line.

Out here, we don't trouble danger
until it arrives at our feet.

People say you can count the rattles
in sets of 2 or 3 to know a snake's age,

but I wonder about time. A birth button
is what they have before their rattles grow.

I like to think that all it took
was the button to be pressed,
then presto, rattlesnake.

I once thought I could remember
my own birth. My screaming punctuality—

I want to say the word *death*
in relation to myself

but it feels like even breathing
the word could take me out nowadays.

Time accelerates. Each day
feels like a footprint of the last.

A hawk swoops into the sorghum
brings a field mouse into the sky.

Out here, there is no death button.

Death often comes quickly
without the mercy of a shout.

Limbo

> *"The world of dew*
> *is a world of dew—*
> *and yet—and yet"*
>
> *~ Kobayashi Issa*

What filters
through the eyelids'
limpid grey
beyond the wet
pink rims & tape?
Does the light
scatter & sprinkle,
opalescent as diatoms,
each time the nurses
turn you gently
as a newborn?

//

Gently, the nurses
turn you, born anew
your eyes inhale
everything in this

blurred hive
of white coats
& blue tunics.
Later, moonlight
dresses the walls,
but for you,
every hour
strikes midnight.

//

Midnight strikes
every hour,
compresses time
into the push
& pull of pain
& opiate—all
that ribbons
through this body
that is no longer
your own.

//

No longer.
Your body diverts
any impulse
to recall *before*
& instead focuses
on breathing
now and *here*.
You whirl in & out

this godless shell
of glass & mask,
as the storm
settles in
your body.

//

What storms
through your body
& ripples through
each ear: susurrus
of gauze & sheet,
soft soles on tile,
crescendo of nurses'
voices, the digits'
electronic squall,
the ventilator
clocking each tiny
breath. The body
winters here,
for now.

//

Winters here
in its coat
of thinning skin,
veins sketched
in a glacier's jasmine
hue—except
for the rosary

of stitches above
your left lung.
The body's sentence
stretched over
the ventilator's
metre. One month:
all possible futures
in flux.

//

The influx of
impossible futures.
One month to witness
the fierce unmaking
of your anatomy.
The lungs shudder
with pure intent,
hauling oxygen
into the concaved
chest. How it
unspools & pools
& exits. We keep vigil
even as you hover
nearer *hail Mary*
than *hallelujah*.

//

Nearer *hail Mary*,
held captive in
this mad rupture,

saddled with
a weight of tubes.
We have bled out
our usefulness
& so we wait,
spectators of
sickness' detritus.
How did I
not know
our bodies are
complex elegies
in motion.

//

Our bodies complex:
elegies in motion,
each detail immense.
So much less
of the body,
so much
more to love,
as your mind floats
unanchored
in a froth
of unmemory.

//

In a froth
of unmemory
the mind

unanchored
as the shadow
of words faltering
on your tongue.
The incision
in your throat
overflows wit
h
the unsayable—
all your language
in limbo.

//

In limbo—all
our language.
I hypothesize
how many
outcomes
you can outrun.
Flattened
onto a screen,
I sense how
your body weighs
each setback
& the viscera
sticks like resin.

//

Like resin,
the viscera.

But I will not
sermon over
your body yet.
Let breath
become flint,
become spark.
Let it gather
in waves.

I cannot fable
the ending
I want.

And yet.
How the wind sirens
through the trees.

And yet. How
the cut roses
glisten.

DYLAN SMITH

Notes on Grieving Gary

I

Uncle Art called from his cabin in the Catskills with a beer in his lap. I could hear the beer in his lap in his voice, and so told him I have no vision; no taste or aesthetic, or even any real aspiration, and in this way hope to absorb some permanence as his apprentice. Absorption by sober observation, I promised him—I *pleaded* him—though even his laugh had some of his lap-beer in it. He said something about permeability. About how everything has it—*like even plastic bottles*—but I'd drunk so many beers myself by then, the details didn't maintain their keep. So I'm starting this journal per Art's suggestion. Entry #1: Gary's jar of paper stars. Old love notes Gary wrote and tore first into strips for me before folding each note nightly, or as into stars before he leapt—or how after Art's call I dreamt of birdsong. Something in that melody resonates in me still, though I'm unsure as to what bird it was. Certainly no city bird; there was salt in the air around its singing, and some sea mist in it, and so in my sleeping I must've manifested some missed calls from Mom. She left me several voicemails, most as reminders to start with this therapist Art's found for me upstate. My childlike life. I leave everything I've ever loved in the city tomorrow morning.

II

Uncle Art's eyes are the color of cold water. A kind of wincing blue, and so I tell him he's looking a bit like John Berryman with his big anguished beard and his glasses. Same old rust-tortured truck idling outside the bus station. Beyond the reservoir, then the river bridge, we wound our way up into wooded mountain pastures. *These mountains are a billion years old*, Art said. Lap-beers in our laps; green bottles gleaming through the blue mountain air. *This rock is one of the oldest formations on earth.* Tonight—for what's to be my Entry #2—my hope is for eyes that will blue as durably as Art's through what's left of August and this heat. The way all of his homeowners love him—*Saint Art!*—their homely handyman living all alone inside his holy little cabin in the woods. Art suggests I spotlight just one job per Entry, *so as not to over-work it*, so tonight I've chosen the garden gate we built behind the Glasshouse; sixteen cedar slats cut to size and wired to keep the deer from *seeping* in—Art's word. He says deer will seek the paths of least resistance, and pass through yards like water, and he explained that the exciting work—*the emergency work*—is to come with changes in the weather. Herons lift out from lily ponds and from the depths of these reflections; deepest greens I've ever seen, and no time yet to call back Mom. Art's lent me his star guides, his birding books. He says the essence of weather is change—or is water. As woodsmen we're to work late and wait calmly for what's to come, by which he seems to mean the griev-ing light of morning, or maybe the *migrating grace* of birds—or maybe he just means winter.

III

Uncle Art is partial to certain trees, though his preference is for
the catalpa leaning outside the Stonehouse. Its leaves are as *big
as bibles*, which make for ample shade, so between jobs Art likes
to park his truck beneath it. A lot of talk radio. A lot of *neighbor-
grown* tomatoes mangled onto *neighbor-made* bread. Today—having
caulked a handful of holes in a church's cedar siding, holes *bored
back in spring* by the carpenter bee—Art formed fists to show
off the size of the catalpa's showy white flowers. Art's truck
radio announced a new space telescope, one capable of captur-
ing the formation of time's first stars. "The very beginnings of
creation," the chief scientist said. "The first moments of God's
firmament—his handiwork—light from thirteen billion years
back—," but before the program finished, Uncle Art explained
how the power steering had gone out on his tractor. *An impos-
sible repair alone*, he said, *and it's been hung up in the trails since spring.*
So together we torqued at tractor bolts, hands aching in a half-
formed trench, and in the fragrance of ferns and hydraulic fluids
and mud, and as Art rode the tractor home—starlings and safety
lights flashing in shallow water—I followed behind him obedi-
ently, thinking, God, Gary would have loved it here. Barns as
permanent as stars; stars as permanent to me as these mountains.
Tonight's Entry #3 ought to be kept a secret from Mom in that
this therapist Art's found for me—*her name is Diane*—she's avail-
able exclusively through a hotline for suicide prevention. Art's
written her extension on my wrist using permanent ink. He says
we're to call Diane if ever we're feeling on the bridge.

IV

Uncle Art's is a mind steeped in scientific reasoning and myth. To showcase the stars through summer's end, he stowed our twin-sized cots onto the screened-in porch *like camping*. From our cots we can see Cassiopeia—its mid-peak pointing true-north over the moonlit pines and mountains—and on Sundays Art wakes with a sigh of Sisyphean patience. Somehow our hangovers haven't permeated his momentum. *Potential energy is energy positioned*, Art read to me today. *Say your tree is standing—say your tree is leaning even—its potential energy is that it's standing still*. So on Sundays, smelling the week's fresh bread, I sometimes try to stir in time to sit for Art's radio shows and his reading. This week he was reading old journals—*foraging for firewood that's adequately seasoned*—and, summoning last spring, spoke of the two *storm-felled* maples that smote the Stonehouse well. But those trees aren't aged enough, Art says. *All those trees are still too green*. So instead we climbed to where, through the temporary scent of two September evenings, we sawed and split an anguished, fallen oak Art found off the trails above the river bridge. Art says the act of stacking firewood is a sort of self-care, and tonight he opened a package from Mom. Inside was a coat—a small, sandy coat still smelling of the coast—and to end Entry #4: Mom wrote us both short notes. A seasonal release has reddened the sail of falling leaves out here, and my skin still smells of gasoline and oak silt—and according to Uncle Art's radio, a hurricane is coming. *A concentration of hurricanes*, he corrects me. So our cots are back inside tonight, and Art's just switched to whiskey, and now he's proposed we start autumn's first fire using Gary's paper stars as our kindling.

V

Uncle Art has me micro-dosing apples. Ripe-red windfalls from an abandoned orchard behind the Glasshouse, and tonight he says these slivers he sliced for me are the same *method he suffered for stone fruit*. In preparing our properties for the storms to pass—all our *weekenders* had already *fled to Florida*—Art and I spent several evenings servicing generators. One night, as the sunset reddened the rust at the edges of Art's truck, a herd of thick-necked deer trickled about the garden gate we built behind the Glasshouse. That generator's engine is enormous; it's fastened to brilliant, blue formations of rock. "The observable universe comprises a fraction of what is there," a radio scientist said. Art replaced the generator's spark plugs, changed the oil. He connected black cables to its battery, and charged it with the idling energy in his truck. "Dark energy, dark matter—our universe is expanding faster than the speed of light—," and wandering off into the crisp, mid-autumn cool of that orchard, I watched a flock of waxwings feeding. According to Uncle Art's birding book, cedar waxwings will *regularly regurgitate chokecherries* into the open throats of their youth—and I really like Diane. Her voice is like the silhouette of some great mountain. I have climbed through it into my memory, where through eight cold, gray city winters, Gary and I absorbed each other's heat beneath the orange cotton comforts of his childhood sheets. Diane has found symbols to solace my grief. For Entry #5: Art says heat isn't really a *visually observable thing*; he says heat's wavelengths are *vaster* than visible light. "October can be a brutal month," Mom wrote to Art in her note. I folded mine into a star; I keep it in the pocket of my coat. "Take care out there with your Uncle."

VI

For Art, work is a form of ritual. These patterns and repeti-
tions—the observable days, their dawns in sequence—a kind
of meaning-making. "When you arrive at the pattern before it's
repeated, you arrive at yesterday," Diane said to me this morning.
It is November now. I can hear the pinched crinkle of Diane's
plastic bottle every time she sips her water. "The present mo-
ment then, is what permeates—it's the ways these patterns are
not repeated that will make a moment apparent." So when after
the hurricane winds had passed, and a dislodged catalpa limb had
fallen through the Stonehouse roof, it was the homeowner's insis-
tence we fell Art's *favorite leaner*—this tremendous, dangerous dif-
ference—that made the present moment more permanently ap-
parent. Let Entry #6 be this diagram Art's drawn for me. A dull
carpenter's pencil on a four-by-four; lap-beer after lap-beer after
lap-beer in his lap—it's supposed to show how a tree is felled.
Turns out great trees are just like bridges, Art said grievously. *Take the
Tacoma Narrows—Puget Sound—1940. Great bridges get felled for their
resonance with great winds, too.* I told him, Art, maybe you ought to
call Diane. He calls his whiskey *hooch*—moonshine—an owl's
nocturnal call. We're both of us looking a bit worse for wear. On
Art's birthday, I dressed like an owl for Halloween. An Eastern
Screech. I glued Uncle Art to eggshells and sticks. I called him
my Big Uncle Nest. We went into town together, but decimated a
deer on our way back up. It pulled itself to the shoulder—streak-
ing—choking on its last cherry-colored breaths. Art did what he
had to do to end it. His rusted truck leaked green. I screeched.

VII

Uncle Art plans for the catalpa tree to be felled on Christmas
Day. He says it's to be *dismantled*, then stacked safely to season
outside the Stonehouse, and so I've practiced on several hol-
lowed trees—ash trees bored-dead already by an *invasive emerald
bug*. What if at its edges, time reverses? What if once seen—
captured, processed—time just ceases? Art replaced the truck's
ruined radiator already, though sometimes I still find tufts of
fawn fur mangled to the grill in green. According to the radio,
tonight's to be the season's first frost. Into every light he ever
leapt, Gary's body always hovered. *You should think of your tree as a
door*, Art said beside his fire. *A big dangerous door—and your cuts are
to function as its hinges.* Inside the Glasshouse, the big hand of a big
clock trembles in tremendous, celestial circles. But no one is ever
inside to see it. In the night sky outside it, constellations streak
clockwise beyond our telescopes and satellites, and Diane says,
"Grief—with time, with work—will ease. Will cease." Tomorrow
will be Sunday. Uncle Art will be reading. I will be eating bread
and birding through binoculars—another chorus of waxwings
through the cabin window—and Art will say something about
the cedar trees. About their berries being birdseed. About how
the migration habits of waxwings have changed with the warm-
ing earth—and into the sunlight Art will stand. Art will leap.
Look, Uncle Art will say. *Look—come look.* Morning's mournful
light will maintain a single shadow inside that room. At its edges,
the shadow will tremble and shake. *That's energy—look, this hovering
you see is making heat.* Art will press his hand against the glass; his
hand will absorb the observable heat. And Gary will be there too.
Gary will be everywhere.

CARELLA KEIL

"Message in a Bottle"
Edited digital photography, 2022

This piece is part of a photo series depicting the organic nature of time, time flattened and distilled on a cellular level. "Message in a Bottle," with its sea glass green color and translucent sheen, embodies the concept of lost memories and thoughts that, once embraced by time, dissolve. Thin spinal lines make up the backbone of this piece, a neural network conveying and shattering emotional memories. Somewhere in this slice of the fourth dimension, a message is retained.

RACHEL MALLALIEU

Sometimes I Still Get Hungry

When I was young, I learned
to stare at the ground
when entering a crowded room—

my skin too tender to bear the raking
eyes of men. And because I was beautiful,
I was hungry and gorged on pho

and Olive Garden breadsticks.
No one cares if you stuff your face
when you are young and pretty.

Now I only eat egg whites and almonds
and no one cares to watch me
gobble a blueberry.

When I look in the mirror,
I recognize my eyes—still green
and dark lashed.

But the corners of my mouth
sag when I smile and I tell
the mirror *that is not me.*

But this face is now my face
and my son will leave
me soon. I miss him

even though he's downstairs
devouring hummus and pita
and Muscle Milk.

Sometimes I look at my son
and only see the imprint
he burns behind my eyes.

NATHAN KING

Awake at 2:58 AM Anticipating Eruption

My brother is becoming a bomb. I lie awake while cicadas scream, his wires crossing, sparks hissing. He strums strings and creates such beautiful sounds; I wish they would wet the gunpowder in his head. But he taps at computer keys, and I imagine he's twisting himself into a rectangular shape with knobs and buttons, preparing for the worst.

When he comes down for dinner, he looks just like a boy, the younger brother I've always known. Our parents won't hear the ticking from his bedroom next door. The constant thrum. They accept silence at face value and ignore the rapid beat of his heel on the vinyl kitchen floor as he pushes food around on his plate and dodges questions about his day. We return to our rooms; I ache to defuse the weapon next door, but we come from a tradition of sitting and waiting.

At one point, our parents will take my brother to a factory where he'll be dismantled and put back together. While he's away, our parents will say he's busy getting better. I'll cry after Thanksgiving dinner because he will be busy getting better. He will forget to turn twenty-one because he's busy getting better.

He'll become strictly boy-shaped again. The bomb pieces will slough onto the dirty carpet of his bedroom floor in a riotous clatter, some hidden among dirty laundry or scraps of garbage.

But he'll gather and keep them tucked away, and some nights he'll tinker and toy and balance them on outstretched limbs, unsure where he exists anymore on the spectrum between life and liability.

Eventually, my brother will snap fully into one state or the other. He could be a boy who someday becomes a man. Maybe he'll move away from home and forget those jagged bomb pieces, hidden beneath old clothes and tattered shoes. Maybe he'll never know how many of my own I've collected and shoved under every damp rug I could find. Or maybe he will dislodge us from sleep in a brilliant flash of blazing light. A hole wrenched in our home, an ascension, a frantic and burning escape.

V.A. BETTENCOURT

Frog Prince Flops Under Scrutiny

Why would it not? All data denoted amphibian.
Even the hypothesis seemed preposterous.

They thought Princess would fall for the fantasy
that a frog could become a prince—the gall.
She set out to dissect their premise in an experiment:

Testable hypothesis: a frog is a frog is a frog.
It is not a transformer.

Predictions: Care, charm, and desire will
not cause it to metamorphose.

Experiment: frog first observed in control condition
devoid of delusion. It was then coaxed, cajoled and catered to
in test conditions designed to optimize and refine. Coaxing
triggered subject's propensity to bolt. Cajoling captured its
attention but sustained it only at increasing doses. Catering
enhanced toadish traits such as brazenness, self-centeredness,
and reclusiveness (except with respect to breeding).

Observations: anatomy characteristic of cold blooded
vertebrate. Overlap with select homo sapiens limited to
camouflage and toxicity. While at times beguiling,
specimen was non-responsive to stimuli;
no transformation or regal traits spotted.*

*Participant known as 'wicked fairy' claims
to have glimpsed the frog as a prince. Data discarded
as confounding factor after fairy was found
to have been under the influence of ecstasy.

Conclusion: no transmogrification detected.
The frog was just a frog.
Resources reallocated to fruitful pursuits.

CINNAMONE WINCHESTER AND SEBASTIÀN UNGCO

"tanggal"
Digital comic drawn using simulated dry brushes. 2022

"tanggal" was initially written as a poem inspired by the penang-galan folklore of Malaysia. In choosing the penanggalan as the vessel for a hybridised exploration of change and its cyclical nature, both Ungco and Winchester hope to inspire a wider interest in her myth, as well as the other quietly enduring creatures of Southeast Asia.

tanggal

illustrated by Sebastiàn Ungco
written by Cinnamone Winchester

amma's warning went like this:
to keep the penanggalan at bay, shatter glass in your hands
and strew the debris,
and strip thorns
from
tender flesh.
pluck pandanus from their palms
you are no ghost hunter;
you are no hero.
pray that she is reckless,

that she will snag her heart
on the hooks at
your window —
that she will turn away
from your locked doors
and
overlook
its seams.

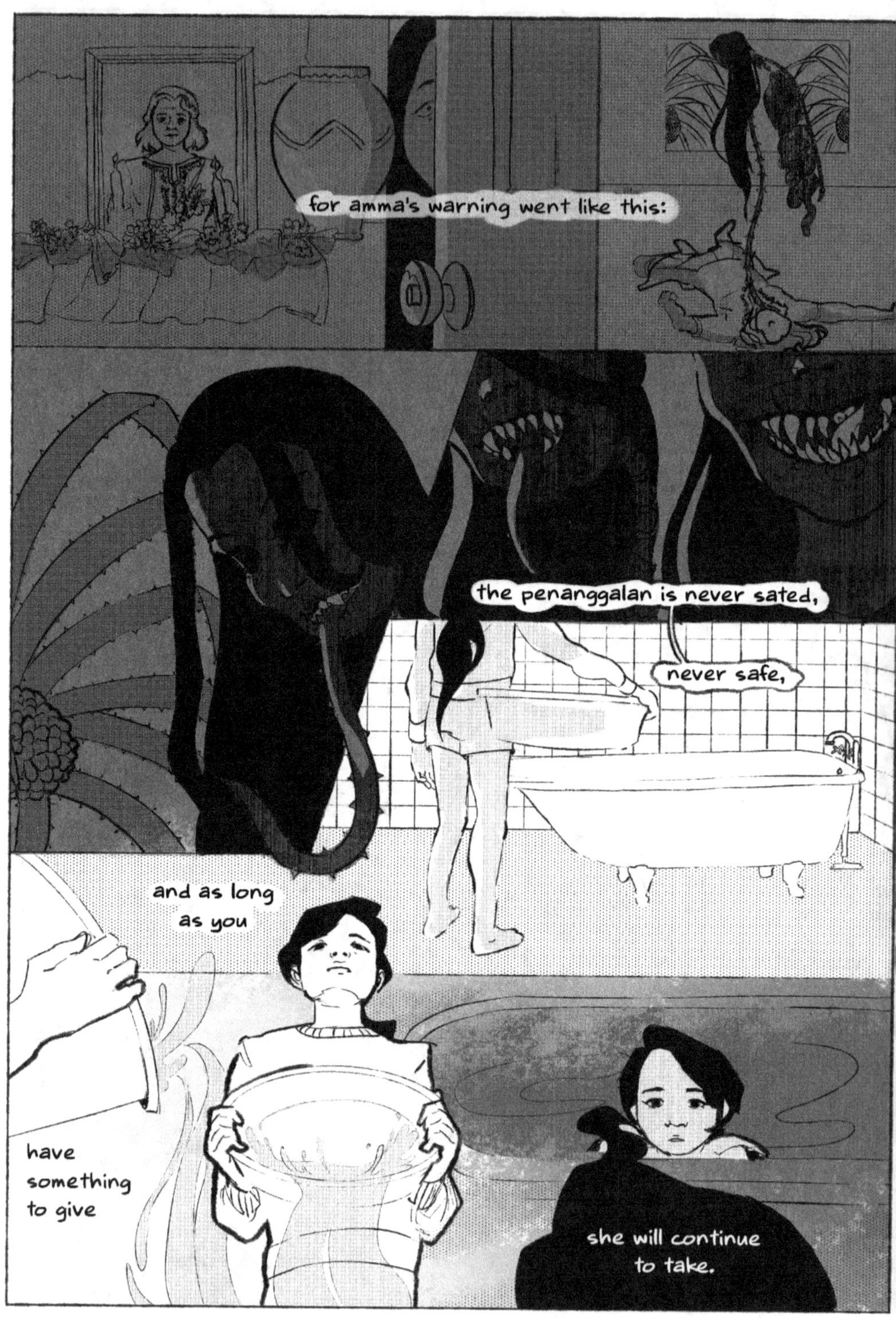

for amma's warning went like this:

the penanggalan is never sated,

never safe,

and as long
as you

have
something
to give

she will continue
to take.

and yet,
there are, i think,
only so many times
you can rearrange your body—
raze your crime scene to the ground
and build a house of bones —

until there is nothing left that you,
intruder,
have the right to call your own.

Across Dark Waters

I know she knows her daughter is dead. If she were a first-time mother, I could imagine she might not understand the difference between a dead baby and one that is simply unresponsive. But she nursed a son eight years before. And she tried to care for her niece after her sister died, but that baby died too. In fact, in this population, 70% of newborns die. Death, unfortunately, is familiar.

It is July 27, 2018, and *The Seattle Times* has broken the story that Tahlequah—known as J35 by killer whale scientists—is still carrying the body of her dead calf three days after giving birth. The calf was the first to be born alive in several years in this endangered population of Southern Resident orcas. She lived for only 20 minutes in the cold waters of the emerald, island-dotted, Salish Sea off the coast of Washington. Tahlequah is now swimming 60 to 70 miles a day, keeping her baby's body afloat.

Although the machines told me hours before that he no longer had a heartbeat, in 2014, four years before Tahlequah, I labored and delivered my son Rhys just as I would have a live baby. I held his eight pounds just as close. Still and close. It was three weeks before his due date.

Many in grief have eloquently tried to pen this emotion, one symptom of which, ironically, is to strip us of words that even begin to trace its precarious outlines.

A hollowing.

A gutting.

An ending in time.

A window blown through them.

Wave-like paroxysms.

An insidious creeping.

A disorienting world of magical thinking.

I know these assaults well. But I also found myself standing alone. Initially, I assumed the separation I felt was from Rhys. One of the most painful moments was finally letting Rhys's body go with the hospital staff to be autopsied. His leaving me was unnatural, like a limb being removed. He was supposed to come home with me. I don't tell most people for fear of their aversion, but I wanted the doctors to put Rhys back inside me. Back where he came from. Back where he belonged.

After Rhys's body was taken for autopsy, my unnamable nature, my unbelonging, began to surface. The hospital didn't know where to put me. I didn't belong on the floor with new mothers and warm babies. I didn't belong on other floors that didn't have postpartum supplies, where they eventually did move me. I had a few stitches from delivery and was still bleeding. I needed the maternity pads they give you after delivery. I needed bed pads. I needed advice on how to manage the milk that my breasts were making. The internal medicine nurse actually asked why I was on her floor. Good question.

We have words for other losses: widow, widower, orphan, divorcée. We have names for the things that change you forever. Although there is a word for a bereaved parent in German, Arabic, Hebrew, and ancient Chinese, in the English language, there is no word for us.

Western culture is squeamish about death. We want it covered, boxed, and professionally "taken care of." We want grievers to be discreet. I learned not to mention Rhys in the grocery store, or at preschool pickup for my other son. I side-stepped around answers because that was the only way to stay a part of the conversation. People wanted me to eat and be normal. People wanted me to move on. I understood—my grief reminded them that such terrible things were possible.

Caitlyn Doughty, a Los Angeles-based mortician, author of *From Here to Eternity*, and founder of The Order of the Good Death, describes in her book how Western culture has come to value "dignity" above all else, which simply translates to "silence, a forced poise, a rigid formality." In the West, according to Doughty, death "must be as if it were not."

––––––––––––––––––

Tahlequah has been carrying her dead calf for seven days. News outlets around the world are now following her story with daily updates and lengthy, scrolling pages of public comments. Scientists report that some members of her pod are taking turns keeping the dead calf afloat, seemingly to let Tahlequah rest and feed.

Carrying a 400-pound carcass is not a passive act—dead calves are not buoyant. Tahlequah and her family members repeatedly take long, deep dives—which require them to prepare with six to seven breaths at the surface—to retrieve the black and white sinking body. Back on the surface, they support the calf on their noses, backs, or pectoral fins, impairing their ability to swim efficiently.

The Whale Museum on San Juan Island releases underwater audio recordings from their hydrophone at Lime Kiln Lighthouse of Tahlequah and her pod using echolocation. Orcas use the clicks, calls, and whistles projected and "echoed" off other objects to find schools of salmon, communicate, navigate along rocky Pacific Northwest coastlines, and stay together as a pod in the often dark and murky waters. Not only do different populations of orcas have different dialects or accents, but even pods within those populations and families within those pods have their own unique languages. Scientists do not know what Tahlequah and her pod are saying—the recordings just prove they are still in the area, together, communicating.

———————————————

Was I sleeping when he died? Was I laughing? Was I eating? Was I cleaning up the urine of his potty-training brother? How could I not have known the exact moment? Felt it in every cell of my body?

Just after Rhys died, a photo of me in the hospital holding Rhys wrapped in the quintessential blue and pink striped hospital blanket circulated among family and friends. I could feel in most responses how much people wanted to take my pain away. However, one response (not sent directly to me) called the photo "so creepy."

Creepy. The dictionary synonyms are *frightening, terrifying, spine-chilling, alarming, shocking, harrowing, horrifying, horrific,* and *nightmarish.* None of those words describe my only moments holding my son.

I held him against my cheek. I wanted to remember his smell. I wanted to remember every inch of him. At one point his lips parted and I heard a soft, saliva sound. I remember truly entering a magical alternate world. *I knew it! He isn't dead. The machines are wrong. The twenty doctors and residents and nurses cycling through the room are all wrong. My family members who are also doctors are wrong. Everyone is wrong. The very pillars of Western medicine are cracking and falling...*

Creepy. The word rang in my ears for months. Perhaps it still does. Like a hospital flat-lining beep that needs to be switched off.

Orcas have a gestation period of 15 to 18 months—almost twice that of a human—so they can give birth only every three to five years. Researchers studying the J, K, and L pods of the Southern Resident Orca population say that when Tahlequah gave birth in 2018, it had been many years since there had been any viable offspring.

The Southern Resident Orca, *Orcinus orca*, has been federally listed as endangered since 2005. During the '60s and early '70s, the main threat to the whales was captivity; 45 whales were taken to parks worldwide and 13 others died during their capture. Now the whales are facing three threats to their survival: water pollution, ship traffic and noise, and lack of enough Chinook salmon. Scientists tell the news outlets that if they had to guess the reason for Tahlequah's baby's death, it would be Tahlequah's malnutrition. Research shows that a calf's chance of survival depends greatly on a good salmon run that year. Researchers are already closely watching another member of Tahlequah's pod, a four-year-old named Scarlet, or J50, who appears to be starving. The Lhaq'temish of the coastal Lummi Nation may try to feed her live salmon.

When I came home from the hospital, I sat on the bed next to my living, two and a half-year-old son, Balen. And Balen knew. Balen knew he didn't get to come to the hospital like we had talked about for months. He saw me come home with no one in the car seat. He sat with me in bed and asked what happened to Pom-Pom. Pom-Pom was the name he gave his brother when we asked for ideas. Although it never became a true contender, the name stuck in our everyday conversation.

"Is Pom-Pom still in there?" he asked, staring at my deflated midsection.

"No, Pom-Pom is not in there anymore," I said.

"Where is he?" Balen asked.

"He came out of my tummy, but he was dead."

"Why?" he asked.

"We don't know," I said.

"Are you sad?" Balen asked. This time he made eye contact.

"I am sad. Daddy is sad. Everyone is sad."

"Is there another baby in there?" he asked.

"No," I said.

And that's often the way it was with him. It was shocking—enough to make me choke. But I appreciated that he didn't beat around the bush hoping I would give him information for which he wasn't brave enough to ask.

It is not unprecedented for an orca to carry a dead infant. There are many records of toothed whales (like orcas), baleen whales, and dolphins carrying dead infants. In most cases,   the mother carries the body, but sometimes the carrier is a close female relative, occasionally a male relative, and often the individual is accompanied by one whale to an entire pod, which scientists label in their reports as "bystanders."

Sometimes this happens in captivity. In 1994 at Point Defiance Zoo in Tacoma, Washington, a mother beluga named Mauyak gave birth to a daughter who died 20 minutes later—her second calf to die in two years. The zoo staff removed the infant's body from the pool. The mother, after delivering the placenta, carried the placenta for 10 hours before zoo staff removed it. She then carried a pink buoy with rope attached (which she had never done before) for several months.

Most cases of wild marine mammals carrying dead infants last a few hours to a few days. Likely there are many in the vast ocean that humans never witness. At nine days, The Center for Whale Research says, as far as they are aware, Tahlequah is setting a record.

In the months following Rhys's stillbirth, I sometimes felt envious of people who had a visible ailment or scar. I wished that everyone knew what happened because I often felt like I had to lie to be part of normal society. Usually, I could get by just saying the truth in my own head.

"Do you just have one child?"

"Yes." (No, one died.)

"Is Balen your only child?"

"Yes." (No, one died).

"Do you want more children?"

"Maybe." (I had one, but he died).

"I can't wait to never be pregnant again."

"Uh-huh." (If you are lucky.)

I often felt like two different people trying to navigate the world. There are things you simply cannot say. If you do, expect to be left alone at the buffet table or by a window with a row of succulents.

"What can I get you?"

(My baby died.) "A grande, nonfat latte, please."

"Regular mail or priority?"

(My baby died.) "Just regular mail."

"Aren't you glad it isn't as humid as it was last week?"

(My baby died.) "Last week was awful."

"Do you have plans today?"

(My baby died.) "No."

"How are you?"

(My baby died. My baby died. My baby died.) "OK…you know."

There is only one answer to every question in the universe.

Sometimes, my conversational-side-stepping failed. At a baby shower a year later, I forgot to stay within the traditional lines of diaper-cake-silliness and premature joy.

"The other morning I couldn't feel anything, but then boom! I felt an elbow!" said the mother-to-be, giggling, echoed by the guests.

"Keep counting those kicks," I said, smiling, but clearly serious. The silence was acute, like a papercut. Flickers of horror were swept away with face-framing bangs and smoothed from Anthropologie blouses. I regretted saying it. The baby would most likely be fine and the mother didn't deserve to be afraid. But I also didn't regret saying it. I would have given anything to have had someone remind me the day before Rhys died to count his kicks.

One of the most helpful books I read shortly after Rhys's death was *Finding Hope When a Child Dies: What Other Cultures Can Teach Us* by Suki Miller, Ph.D. It is an unassuming paperback, written in 2002, with only seven Amazon reviews. It does not come up in the initial wave of books when you search about stillbirth and children dying, and the cover is less than inviting. In many other cultures, there are rituals and stories that surround the death of infants or children. The Yakurr people in the rainforests of Nigeria believe the child's spirit stays by the body after it dies to judge whether it is worth returning to the same parents. If the parents are grieving and sad, then the child will know it was loved and perhaps will consider returning to those parents in a future incarnation.

The babalawo or spiritual leader of the Yoruba people in West Africa consults with their God Ifa to find out why the child chose to die. Other African tribes take the perspective that certain children were not meant to live; they are "abiku" or born to die. The Karanga people of Zimbabwe bury the stillborn fetus in a gambe jar shaped like a uterus in the grainy sand of the sloping riverbank. In the first rains, when the river rises, the jar is swept away, and the Karanga believe that the child is reborn to another woman on Earth.

The Mahapatras of India are untouchable members of society because they bear the shadow of death—they care for the wrapped bodies of the deceased on the burning ghats, the wide stairway used for cremation leading down to the holy Ganges River. The Mahapatras believe that inherited karma can take a child early, but an Indian astrologer may be able to find the child's spirit and karmic path among the great orbits of the planets and the starry darkness in between.

The Toraja people of Indonesia believe the souls of stillborn children roam the Earth, thirsty for water, drinking dew and raindrops until the soul of their mother comes and takes them to the city of the dead. The Japanese secure the favor of the guardian of the crossroads, Jizo, to help the unborn spirit—mizuko, or child of the water—to cross over the river into the afterworld. Mizuko Jizo statues are everywhere in Japan—visible and part of everyday culture. Parents place little offerings nearby.

The Afro-Brazilian-Catholic Umbanda religion and culture, based mostly in Brazil, say that when a child dies, spirits of the family help him break his ties with the earth and guide him to the spirit realm or back to be reincarnated. The Hopi Tribe of the American Southwest believes a child who dies returns to the house of the parents and waits to be reborn in the next child. If there are no more children, they join their mother at the gates of the underworld when she dies.

Whether I agreed spiritually with the beliefs or traditions of these other cultures did not make a difference to me. What I found in these stories were other women, across time and across extremely different cultures, who were profoundly affected by losing a baby. They needed explanations. They needed to believe their baby was OK, wherever he or she was. They needed to still belong.

It has been just over two weeks. Tahlequah is still carrying her decaying calf and has traveled almost 1000 miles. Scientists and anthropologists argue heatedly and publicly over whether her actions can be labeled as grief. Deborah Giles, an orca biologist at the University of Washington, tells *The Seattle Times* that Tahlequah's actions could not be interpreted as anything other than grief. But another scientist at the University of Washington tells *The Seattle Times* that we need to be cautious about projecting our own feelings onto the orca.

The scrolling public comments below the daily Tahlequah update have, for weeks, given a glimpse at how divided humanity is over the idea that a whale might be grieving and, more so, what to do about it.

"It's obvious what is happening…this animal is grieving for its dead baby, and she doesn't want to let it go."

"There is a really quick jump to interpreting this behavior as grief."

"What is beyond grief? I don't even know what the word for that is, but that is where she is."

"We have to be cautious about not projecting about how this makes us feel."

"Someone needs to remove the dead calf and dispose of it so the mother can move on."

"Humans need to stay out of this and let nature take its course."

I was informed of many things I had to do after Rhys died. At the top of the list was immediately finding a therapist who would talk me through my grief and deliver me to the other side, ready to reenter society. (Eventually, I did see a therapist, but not until much later, when I was ready to put words together.) Almost every conversation in the first month began with, "Have you found a professional you can talk to?" I could tell it was comforting for family members and friends to know I was processing my grief—but with someone else, behind closed doors. My grief did not belong outside, drying in the warm, second summer winds of October.

Instead of immediately finding a therapist, I bought a portable paper shredder, and Balen and I sat for hours feeding paper into the teeth of the "Gorgosaurus." Could he feel that sometimes I wanted to put myself through the shredder? I don't know. Could he feel that sometimes I wasn't sure how to put my failed-mother self back together, like the confettied documents all around us? Maybe.

Sometimes, Balen and I threw rocks into a muddy, fern-laced stream near our house in Oakland, California. He usually did not acknowledge the weight I was carrying, which made me feel like I might sink into the streambank. But just when I thought that he, too, had finally left me alone in the darkness, he would echo the words in my mind, as if he could hear them.

"Pom-Pom died. And he isn't coming back."

He said this one day as he popped up to the surface in the pool in which we were swimming. It was a month after Rhys died, on a day when I could not understand why summer had not immediately bypassed fall plunging into the deepest winter on record.

"Yes…" I said, my brain clunking and screeching like a dysfunctional machine with bolts and nuts clanging to the ground. As I was trying to figure out what to say, Balen dove back underwater and grabbed his toy dinosaur from the bottom of the pool. In some ways, he was right. That was all that needed to be said.

After two weeks, Tahlequah's calf's body begins to deteriorate, but the whales keep diving into the dark waters, retrieving it, and carrying it with them. Each time Tahlequah dives, she has to make a conscious decision to do it again. And again. And again. The default is to do nothing, and the body will sink away into the depths.

On August 11, 2018, The Center for Whale Research reports that the calf is gone. No one sees the moment the calf's body disappears. Tahlequah and the rest of the pod may have finally defaulted, not retrieving it the last time it sank. Or it may have disintegrated past the point of retrieval and carrying. All we know is that after 17 days and over 1,000 miles of decisions and hard work, something changes.

The relatively new and growing fields of comparative and evolutionary thanatology—the comparative study of non-human animal responses to death and the study of the evolution of human responses to death—are uncovering to what degree many non-human animals understand or behave around death, and how ancient humans evolved a comprehension of death. It used to be an absolute career-ender to consider animal emotions in any scientific study, let alone acknowledge that animal emotions exist. In some fields, it still is taboo.

But the Frans de Waals, Richard Louvs, Jane Goodalls, Carl Safinas, and Barbara Kings out there—you know, the ones that have spent their entire lives studying animals—will tell you that we have much in common with animals, especially highly intelligent, social animals. "Our desire for sharp divisions is at odds with evolution's habit of making extremely smooth transitions," says Frans de Waal. The growing list of animals that have more complex reactions to death—elephants, giraffes, wild horses, peccaries, dolphins, whales, seals, manatees, dingoes, birds, cats, dogs, rabbits, goats, and multiple species of monkeys and apes—stretches long, like evolutionary time, raising questions about humanity's aggressive ownership claim over grief and all other emotions. Other scientists are pushing back, too. "The question of animal emotions" graced the prestigious pages of the leading journal Science in March 2022, arguing for the sentience and emotional intelligence of invertebrates like octopus and lobster.

I wonder what Tahlequah and her pod were saying to each other after carrying a dead calf for over two weeks? Were they trying to convince her to let go? Were they trying to distract her by talking about salmon? Were they telling her she was completely off her rocker and endangering her own survival as well as theirs?

Of course, we can't know what they were saying. But it doesn't really matter, does it? She could hear their echoes across the darkness. She wasn't alone. Why do people need to fight over how to label any of it? Grief? Call it whatever you want. But look at the facts and at her actions and her pod's actions. An incredibly intelligent, highly social species with a customized dialect within a larger whale language altered their normal behavior for 17 days and communicated together while continuously carrying and diving for a decaying, sinking body. That doesn't need a name.

I made my offerings. I was the one who touched the dead and carried him to the banks of the Ganges. I buried him in his jar. I traced his path through sand and stars and now wait for the river's mighty tide. I look for him in raindrops. And I reach down looking for his hand at every gate, at every river, at every crossing. Perhaps there will always be a piece of me there, in the deep darkness of the receding tide, with him.

Barbara King says, "Goat grief, then is not chicken grief. And chicken grief is not chimpanzee grief or elephant grief or human grief." Just because our grief doesn't look the same doesn't mean it isn't there. King pushes this further to say even within species there may be variability in grief that we need to be able to see and accept. "There is no one way to be a chimpanzee or goat or chicken," she says, "just as there is no one way to be human." No, there is no one way to be human.

I am in awe of those—human or non-human—who somehow know exactly what to do when someone they love is in danger of being lost. Because the reality is, sometimes you might have to talk about the only thing she can think about. Sometimes you might have to be an echoing voice she can hear in the darkness. Sometimes, yes, you might even have to descend to dark fathoms with her. But sometimes you might just need to swim next to her until she finds her own way home through the darkness.

Editor's note: for a list of sources used in this essay, please check our online version.

ALBA DELIA HERNÁNDEZ

20 Bars for Vitiligo

1

mami said I was born with the map of
puerto rico on my thigh
a tiny splotch of white on my brown skin

2

by five years old
un lagartijo blanco
along my shins

3

mami picked dandelions from a junkyard
then rubbed my white spots yellow

4

when i was ten
a little girl at a beach pointed at me
asked her mom
what happened to her?
her mom whispered
she got burned because she
wasn't listening

5

an egyptian man in a smoke shop told me
the skin of a snake can cure you

6

in quebradillas
someone (and i curse this number 6)
said that eating liver every day
would cure me
mami made me eat liver every day for a year

7

mami boiled cloves and with a cotton ball
dabbed clove juice on all my spots
i slept with the sweet smell of cloves
the only cure i liked

8

spring/summer/skin
even walking out of my house was hard

9

what the fuck you looking at?

10
winter/fall my favorite seasons
sweaters to cover up my arms

11
when she hits puberty
a vecina tells mami
eso se le va

12
in my teens
weekly ultraviolet treatments $100 a session
my poor mom working two factory jobs

13
i searched the etymology of vitiligo
in the OED
another name for vitiligo—
alba

14
no i'm not contagious

15
a boyfriend invites me to a wedding
when i show up in a short dress
he says *why didn't you wear something*
to cover up your spots
everybody is looking at us

16
a better boyfriend says
if we have kids
he hopes they inherit
my spots

17
there is no cure for vitiligo

18
only radical self-love
the kind that audre lorde speaks of

19
i am all vitiligo white now

20
i miss my spots

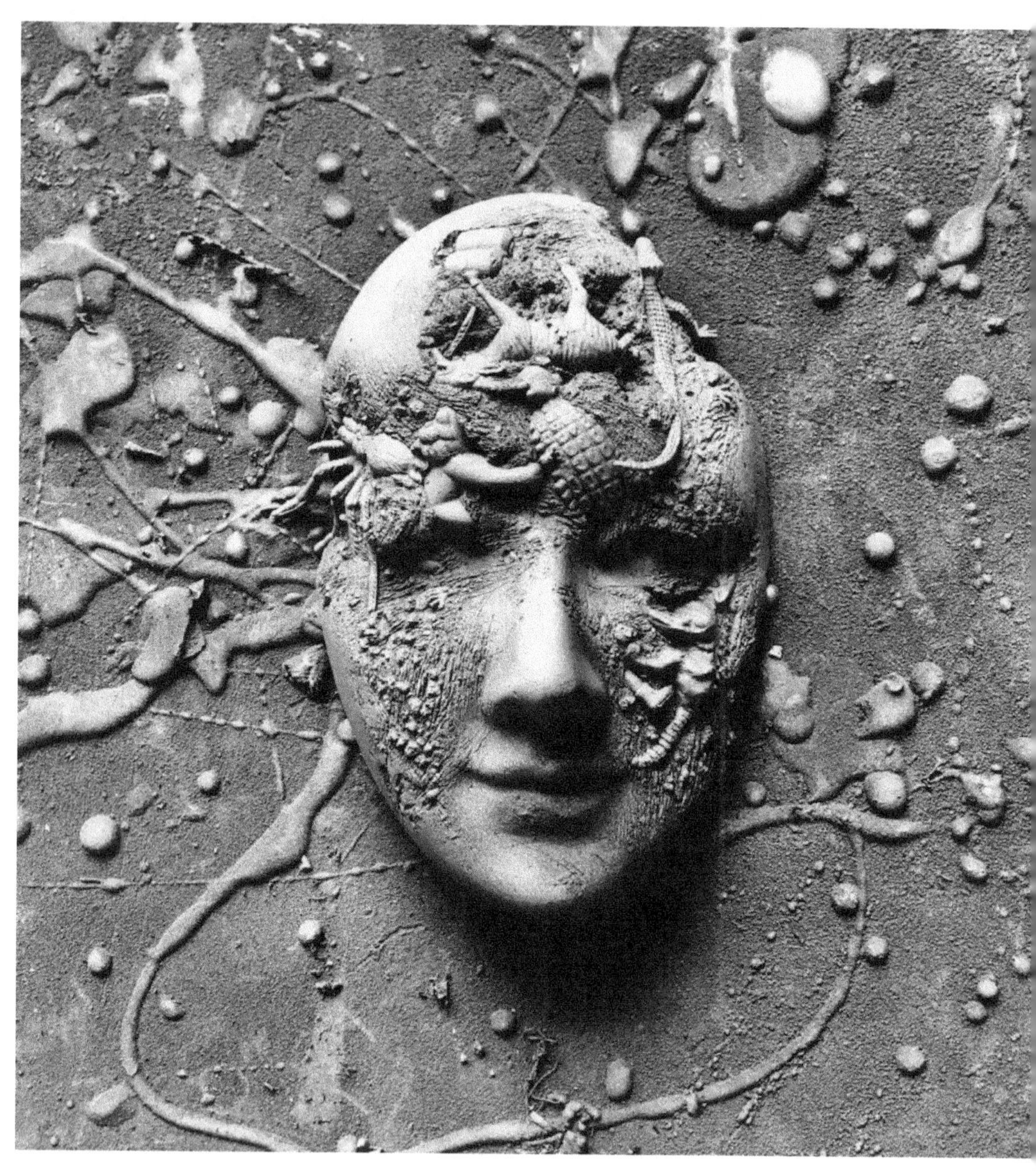

JACK BORDNICK

"Facing It Together"
Mixed media, 12x12x3 inches. Santa Fe, New Mexico, 2021

My works represent what I have accomplished with this art form. I call it my quantum and metaphoric moment, the changing from one form to another. They express and implement my thoughts and feelings, regarding taking risks, without any guarantee of their success….. and to be reflected in these present works, is my goal. The predominant imagery deals mostly with faces of both living and non-living beings and things. They are expressed in these many forms and images and do speak to us in their own languages.These present sculptural images incorporate both surrealistic and mythological and magical imagery, fabricated in mixed media assemblages. They are assembled, disassembled and reassembled.

JADE Y. LIU

Foodsafe

If the doubling time of bacteria spores on white rice
left idling in the cooker is twenty minutes, then I'm a mother

of trillions, rebred every night at the dinner table
with meat velveted so tender nobody

knows the internal temperature
because "thermometers are for white people."

My tongue whets for the salt sweet linger
of weeks-old stock, umami boiled soybean dark

in the belly of an earth-clay pot. These are the things I love.
The crumbling yolk of a third day tea egg from the bamboo basket,

snow mushroom wisps drowned in rock sugar syrup
like ghosts of who we were in that wide, wide ocean.

But in high school I buttercreamed cakes and roasted hollow chickens
and was taught the fridge as sacred—stainless steel utopia

with a two hour entry limit where stragglers are tossed overboard
just to be safe, the compost plumps with over-sharpened cheese,

whey-wet yogurt best before the weekend, the end pieces of bread
left until fungus buds gorge themselves green.

Last year, the white boy I dated flew to Singapore and saw
mostly the toilet. His stomach is weak, māma laughs. Stuffed

with the privilege of leaving flesh on drumstick bones
when bàba has to find the discount corner in supermarkets.

He rescues the rejects, the intestines, livers, and kidneys
crosshatched into flowers for his oil flame wok,

every organ unfurls in five-spice like it remembers
living. And I promise you this: around our table

we bite bones so clean we could build
a paddle, a raft sinewed blood-tight, we waste nothing

because we have had nothing. Our fingers pressed bladeside,
we scrape mold crusts until we find unscarred flesh

and trust the fire to kill enough for our bodies to do
what they have done for dynasties. Every mouthful

a remembrance. Every swallow, resilience.

CONTRIBUTORS

Caitlyn Alario is a queer poet from Southern California. She holds an MFA from Sarah Lawrence College and works as a Teaching Fellow and doctoral student at the University of North Texas, where she reads for *American Literary Review*. Her work has appeared in *Third Coast*, *Vallum Magazine*, *Annulet*, and elsewhere.

V.A. Bettencourt writes poetry and short prose. Her work has appeared or is forthcoming in *Magma Poetry*, *Burningword Literary Journal*, *Roanoke Review* and *SWWIM Every Day*, among others.

Jack Bordnick has been part of this creative art world since he can remember, beginning as a product designer and establishing his own design business in New York, Santa Fe, and Europe.

Alba Delia Hernández is an award winning writer, inspired by Puerto Rico, growing up in Bushwick, and *salsa*, who dances in the hybrid forms of fiction, playwriting and poetry. She was awarded the winner of the 2022 One Festival for her one woman show, *Juana Peña Revisited* and most recently read for the Bushwick Starr's 2023 annual reading series at the Center for Performance Art. She is a recipient of the Bronx Council of the Arts First Chapter Award and earned a Bachelor of Arts degree from Columbia University. Her writing was highly commended in the Gathering of the Tribes Magazine, The Chestnut Review and other publications. She has performed at El Museo del Barrio, The Whitney Museum, Nuyorican Poets Café, En Garde Arts and La Respuesta in Puerto Rico and other venues. She's a passionate yoga teacher, salsa dancer, and videographer who recites speeches by Puerto Rican revolutionaries or moves to songs of resistance. She teaches creative writing to NYC public school students with Teachers & Writers Collaborative.

Armaan Kapur (he/him) is a writer and designer from New Delhi. His short prose has appeared or is forthcoming in *Cutleaf Journal*, *The Reader Berlin*, *Apparition Lit*, *Mason Jar Press*, and *Helter Skelter Magazine*. He is currently pursuing two full-length projects:

a debut novel about existentialism, and a collection of speculative, queer novellas. Find him at armaankapur.com.

Margaret Karmazin is both artist and writer. Her art work, usually done in acrylics, has appeared in *SageWoman*, *The MacGuffin*, *Adirondack Review*, *Ascent*, *Persimmon Tree* and other publications and in shows and galleries in PA, NY and the Caribbean. Her short stories have appeared in literary and SF magazines, including *Rosebud*, *Chrysalis Reader*, *North Atlantic Review*, *Mobius*, *Confrontation*, *Pennsylvania Review*, *The Speculative Edge*, *Aphelion* and *Another Realm*. Her stories in *The MacGuffin*, *Eureka Literary Magazine*, *Licking River Review* and *Mobius* were nominated for Pushcart awards.

Carella Keil is a writer and digital artist who splits her time between the ethereal world of dreams, and Toronto, Canada, depending on the weather. Her art has appeared recently on the cover of *Glassworks 26*, in *Columbia Journal*, *Skyie Magazine*, *Existere*, *The Cafe Review*, *The Storms Journal* and *Door is a Jar*. Instagram.com/catalogue.of.dreams, Twitter @catalogofdream.

Sydney Megan Kim is a recent graduate of Wesleyan University, where she earned her BA in psychology and English. She is the 2018 winner of the Wesleyan University Hamilton Prize for Creativity for her short story, "The Driveway." She currently lives in New York City. This is her first fiction publication. Find her on Instagram @sydneymegankim or Twitter @sydneymkim.

Nathan King is a writer living in New Jersey. They hold an MFA from Sarah Lawrence College and their fiction has previously appeared in *LEVEE Magazine* and *Unstamatic*. In their free time they fill their bullet journal with the color pink, watch horror movies right before bed, and dance to K-pop alone in their room. You can find them on Twitter @nathan___king (3 underscores!).

Jade Y. Liu is a Chinese-Canadian writer and poet from Vancouver, BC. A recipient of the 2020 George McWhirter Prize in Poetry, she was shortlisted for *Arc Poetry Magazine's* 2022 Poem of the Year and won Reader's Choice in *CV2's* 2022 2-Day Poem Contest. She currently studies Law at UBC.

Rachel Mallalieu is an emergency physician and mother of five. She writes poetry in her spare time. Rachel is the author of *A History of Resurrection* (Alien Buddha Press 2022). Some of her recent poems appear in *Nelle, DIALOGIST, West Trestle Review* and *Rattle*.

Oormila Vijayakrishnan Prahlad is an Indian-Australian artist, poet, and improv pianist. Her art has been featured on the covers of several journals including *Amsterdam Quarterly* yearbook, *Pithead Chapel, Two Thirds North, Kissing Dynamite Poetry*, and *Stonecoast Review*. Her work has been nominated multiple times for the Best of the Net. She lives and works in Sydney on the traditional lands of The Eora Nation. Find her @oormilaprahlad and www.instagram.com/oormila_paintings.

Dacia Price is an MFA candidate at Northern Michigan University where she teaches composition and is associate editor for *Passages North*. Her work has appeared or is forthcoming in *DIAGRAM, The Forge Literary Magazine, Pacifica Literary Review, 45th Parallel*, and others. Her writing has been nominated for Best of the Net in both 2019 and 2020 and in 2022 her flash essay "Here // Not Here" won the Roadrunner Nonfiction Prize.

Dylan Smith works in Accord, NY, and is currently working on a novella. Twitter: @dylan_a_smith.

Charlotte Stevenson has a broad writing portfolio ranging from the technical to the creative. She writes for institutions and organizations such as NOAA, USC Sea Grant, the Institute of Science and Policy of the Denver Museum of Natural History, and Scripps Institution of Oceanography. She has published freelance pieces in *Undark, Age of Awareness*, and *The New York Times Online*. She is currently a degree candidate in the Johns Hopkins Advanced Academic Master's Program in Science Writing and has an M.S. and B.S. in Biology from Stanford University, spending many years at Hopkins Marine Station in Monterey, CA.

Sebastiàn Ungco is a South East Asian illustrator and multimedia arts student based in Metro Manila, Philippines. They specialize in hybridizing visual arts and other creative forms which showcase their attraction to the delicate craft of story-retelling. If not freelancing and developing fantasy visuals, they can be found curating their 220th Spotify playlist and daydreaming about animated music videos. Find them on Twitter (@sebisdrawing) and Instagram (@sebc0re).

Laura Villareal is the author of *Girl's Guide to Leaving* (University of Wisconsin Press, 2022). She has received fellowships from the Stadler Center for Poetry & Literary Arts and National Book Critics Circle. Her writing has appeared in *Guernica*, *AGNI*, *American Poetry Review*, and elsewhere.

Cara Waterfall, Ottawa-born and Costa Rica-based, has poetry featured in *Best Canadian Poetry*, *The Ekphrastic Review*, *The Night Heron Barks* and more. She won 1st and 2nd place in *PULPLiterature's* The Magpie Award for Poetry, 2nd place in *Frontier Poetry's* Award for New Poets, *Room's* 2018 Short Forms and 2020 Poetry Contests, and was shortlisted for the 2019 CBC Poetry Prize. She is also a two-time finalist for *Radar Poetry's* The Coniston Prize. She has a diploma in Poetry & Lyric Discourse from The Writer's Studio at SFU and is currently a reader for *Frontier Poetry*. www.carawaterfall.com, @carawaterfall.

Cinnamone Winchester is a Malaysian writer who currently lives on Ngunnawal and Ngambri land, Australia. Her work—which often interacts with fairy tales, myth, and folklore—is featured or forthcoming in *Bossy*, *ANU Undergraduate Research Journal*, *Panorame Press*, and *All Existing Magazine*. For her analysis of queer and postcolonial utopia in *The Chronicles of Narnia*, she received the Gender Institute's 2022 Honours Prize for Excellence in Gender and Sexuality Research. Find her on Twitter @ciniswriting.

Mimi Yang currently resides in Shanghai, but she has lived in Boston and Montreal. Her work has been recognized by the Alliance for Young Artists and Writers and the UK Poetry Society, and appears or is forthcoming in *Palette Poetry*, *BOOTH*, *The Margins*, and else-where.

Grace Zhou is a visual artist based in Alberta, Canada, who aims to create art that prompts the rethinking of occurrences featured in her work. Her work is featured in *Hot Pot Magazine*, *HaluHalo Journal*, *Gaia Literary Magazine*, among others.

Chestnut Review
for stubborn artists

www.ingramcontent.com/pod-product-compliance
Lightning Source LLC
Chambersburg PA
CBHW071349300726
48976CB00006B/1816